# Things We Learned in Organizations ...

# Things We Learned in Organizations …

Keith Grant, PhD
Janis McFaul, PhD
Jeanette Pack, DM, and
Ionie Douglas, DM

iUniverse, Inc.
New York   Bloomington

# Things We Learned in Organizations...

*iUniverse books may be ordered through booksellers or by contacting:*

*iUniverse*
*1663 Liberty Drive*
*Bloomington, IN 47403*
*www.iuniverse.com*
*1-800-Authors (1-800-288-4677)*

*ISBN: 978-0-595-25160-5 (pbk)*
*ISBN: 978-0-595-65045-3 (cloth)*
*ISBN: 978-1-4401-0333-9 (ebk)*

*Printed in the United States of America*

*iUniverse rev. date: 11/19/2008*

To my mother—you always believed in me and encouraged me to shoot for the stars! I am blessed for having you in my corner.

Janis

To my wife, Patricia Grant; my daughter, Janelle Grant; my mother, Eunice Hill; my sisters, Sharon and Michelle, you have always provided me with continued support. Finally, to Dr. Edward Wingard at the Union Institute and University for his quiet leadership. Chapter five is dedicated to Dr. Nancy K. Owens (GM) and Dr. Edward Wingard (Union Institute and University).

Keith

Greatness
By Edgar Guest


We can be great by helping one another;
We can be loved for very simple deeds;
Who has the grateful mention of a brother
Has really all the honor that he needs.

We can be famous for our works of kindness—
Fame is not born alone of strength or skill;
It sometimes comes from deafness and from blindness
To petty words and faults, and loving still.

We can be rich in gentle smiles and sunny:
A jeweled soul exceeds a royal crown.
The richest men sometimes have little money,
A Croesus oft's the poorest man in town.

# CONTENTS

# ACKNOWLEDGMENTS

I would like to thank the following individuals for their long-term support: Steven and Esther Hollings; Evaughn Hopson; Linda Johnson; Billy Burgess; Donald and Charlene Johnson; Brian and Sonia Hopson; Debbie Keith; Melvin Rusher; Jeanette Pack, DM; and Janis McFaul, PhD.


Keith Grant

# FOREWORD

Leadership in the new millennium offers tremendous challenges. Key drivers of these challenges include the fierce competitive marketplace, globalization, new business realities, organizational structures based on business requirements, rapid change driven by innovation, and high expectations from the incoming generation of leaders. Leadership is clearly being redefined and creating opportunities for leaders to have significant business impact that leads to results on the bottom line.

In light of the key drivers, it is imperative to establish an environment that allows ordinary leaders to achieve extraordinary results. A new focus on leadership development and change management creates renewed realities of leadership, in an effort to optimize on building people and organizational capability to drive results, and finally, achieving success through profound leadership practices.

I offer the following definition of leadership: The ability to influence, motivate, and inspire in ways that meet organizational goals and people objectives. Leadership is guiding strategic direction in pursuit of business results. Leadership is focused on both behavior and results. Leadership is about the tasks and the people. Leadership mobilizes resources to accomplishment business objectives. Leadership is the effective use of power to gain the hearts and minds of the organization to achieve competitive advantage in the marketplace.

This book offers a collection of ideas that provide creative insights to change management strategies, the learning organization, and leadership development. It will generate new thinking that will cause the reader to reflect, challenge, and exploit the ideas presented in a manner that may drive a fresh direction in leading and managing people and change.

The foundation of leadership includes a passion for change and provides the energy and focus that can drive an organization. Strong leaders must maximize the full capability of the organization, as well as the people within the organization. The concepts presented demonstrate that leaders can launch the organization on a path for success. This is exciting and invigorating when leaders can tap into the workforce and influence, motivated and inspired to create success for employees and for the enterprise.

Enjoy the journey of leadership, change, and courage.

Victoria E. Jones,
Director, College of Leadership
General Motors Corporation
August 1, 2002

# Chapter One

## Models and Theories for Understanding Change

## Keith Grant

As with all experiences, the experience of change must be contextualized in order to gain understanding and identify appropriate competencies for successfully managing it. Our experiences are understood through frameworks, or paradigms, which have proved to be useful in responding to situations or explaining them. Frameworks are also influenced by our philosophical and theological underpinnings. When a framework no longer proves useful, either in terms of functionality or elucidation, we experience cognitive and emotional dissonance, which provides the motivation to seek new information and adjust our framework. If we fail to make the appropriate adjustments, our framework ultimately works against us. In his book, *Permanence and Change: An Anatomy of Purpose,* Kenneth Burke points out Thorstein Veblen's concept of "trained incapacity," which seems especially relevant to this point. He referred to trained incapacity as "that state of affairs whereby one's very abilities can function as blindness. If we had conditioned chickens to interpret the sound of a bell as food-signal, and if we now rang the bell to assemble them for punishment, their training would work against them. With their past education to guide them, they would respond in a way which would defeat their own interests. Veblen generally restricts his concept to the case of businessmen, who, through training in competitive finance, so built their orientation of right and wrong ways of responding that they could not see serious possibilities in any other system of production." Veblen's concept explains the development of ineffective paradigms that are created through continued antiquated training.

Our current framework for understanding change has proven to be ineffective with organizational change. The past twenty years of business have been uncharacteristically marked by substantial change. Today, change is no longer an event, or series of events, but a new environment marked by chaos that requires new ways of thinking and working. It seems unreasonable, therefore, that workers repeatedly exposed to dynamic levels of change should have built up a tolerance for change or, at least, strategies for effective change management. Workers today more than ever should be able to handle change. They have been exposed to thousands of hours of training for managing their attitudes, emotions, stress, and time. These are the strategies that have been taught since the late seventies and generally accepted as the way to effectively manage change. Yet change management is still a major issue in organizations today. Joseph and Jimmie Boyett in their book, *The Guru Guide: The Best Ideas of the Top Management Thinkers,* put it this way: "For all the CEO huffing and expensive [change] guru puffing, nothing much changed and changes that were accomplished rarely lasted or reaped the results promised by their advocates. By most estimates, 50 to 70 percent of all corporate change initiatives launched in the 1980s and 1990s failed to achieve their objectives. More specifically, one survey in the mid-1990s found that two-thirds of all corporate restructuring efforts failed to achieve the outcomes they were designed to achieve, while leading practitioners of reengineering reported that their success rates among Fortune 1,000 companies were well below 50 percent and perhaps as low as 20 percent." People still resist change at all levels within the organization. Worker satisfaction remains low, and the psychological employment contract continues to be based on distrust. In order to understand the failure of change management strategies we must examine not only the strategies themselves but also the framework the strategies are based upon.

The traditional framework for understanding change has been the grieving process, made popular by the work of Elisabeth Kubler-Ross in 1969. Kubler-Ross worked with terminally ill patients and noted that people who have been informed that they are terminally ill go through several cognitive and emotional stages before accepting their fate (figure 1). The same stages have been identified in the grieving process over the loss of a loved one. The work completed by Kubler-Ross and others laid the foundation for understanding loss, whether of life, identity, or job. The grieving process became our framework for understanding what workers needed to "work through" in order to "get on with their lives." Over time, the grieving framework has been modified and molded in various ways to understand human resistance to organizational change.

Stage One: Shock and Denial
Stage Two: Anger
Stage Three: Bargaining
Stage Four: Depression
Stage Five: Acceptance
Figure 1

RIGHT Associates, a national outplacement and transition consulting organization, uses the Transition Cycle model popularized by Dennis Jaffe and Cynthia Scott in the late 1980s. The Jaffe and Scott model identifies four stages individuals move through when experiencing change. Although RIGHT Associates deleted the four directional indicators of the original model, the four skills identified for dealing with change remain the same. According to RIGHT Associates, "Each skill can help people move through a phase of the transition process." The skills identified by RIGHT Associates are explained in the following way.

| STAGE | SKILL | EXPLANATION |
|---|---|---|
| Denial | Notice | "The reality of the situation. Ask what has happened and why." |
| Resistance | Feel | "What is going on inside of you? Understand the reasons for it." |
| Exploration | Reframe | "Your thinking. Look for the opportunities that are available to you." |
| Commitment | Focus | "Your energy where you can make the greatest difference." |

It is easy to see that the strategies suggested by RIGHT Associates focus on the grieving framework, which is the basis for Jaffe and Scott's model.

Another approach to understanding change is the Personal Transition Cycle. This model is currently used to train professionals throughout the country in change management. The model focuses on the same emotional components defined by Kubler-Ross, but it is applied to the process of personal transition. The model differentiates between impact and denial, integration and acceptance. RIGHT's explanation of the model states grief as an inevitable element of change. "Change creates an ending. This includes job change. Endings produce grief. This is inevitable. Grief is not a linear process. Grief is cyclical, goes through stages, and must be processed." The model indicates everyone must work through a phase of depression when experiencing change. The grieving framework supports the concept that depression is associated with change. This concept is held by many popular authors such as Scott Peck. "All change is a kind of death, and all growth requires that we go through depression." The depression implication is reasonable if the grieving framework is applied as the basis for understanding change. It is also reasonable that the suggested strategies for successfully working through change tend to be the same strategies for successfully working through the grieving process. These conclusions are reasonable but not necessarily accurate or functional as demonstrated by the current success rate of organizational change (figure 2).

Step One: Impact
Step Two: Denial
Step Three: Anger
Step Four: Bargaining
Step Five: Depression
Step Six: Integration

Figure 2

William Bridges's transition model was initially presented in his book *Transitions* and developed further in his later work, *Managing Transitions: Making the Most of Change*. Bridges identifies three stages of change: the ending, neutral zone, and beginning (figure 3). Each phase has unique characteristics though the phases overlap.

Ending ⟶ Neutral Zone ⟶ New Beginning

Figure 3

The ending stage has "four different aspects of the natural ending experience: disengagement, disidentification, disenchantment, and disorientation." Bridges's neutral zone has three "activities or functions" associated with the "emptiness of the state." These include surrender to the emptiness, seeing the emptiness as a source of self-renewal, and seeing the perspective the emptiness provides. Bridges identifies the neutral zone stage as requiring completion prior to moving to the beginning stage. "It is when the endings and the time of fallow neutrality are finished that we can launch ourselves out anew, changed and renewed by the destruction of the old-life phase and the journey through the nowhere." Bridges's key to understanding change is seeing change and transition as separate issues and loss as the main issue. "Change occurs when something new starts or something old stops, and it takes place at a particular point of time. But transition cannot be localized in time that way, since it is the gradual psychological process through which individuals and groups reorient themselves so that they can function and find meaning in a changed situation." He identifies six categories of loss associated with transition: "Loss of attachments, turf, structure, future, meaning, and control." It is when the neutral zone is examined that we find Bridges's approach flows from the grieving process associated with death and dying. "Although the neutral zone is no longer widely recognized, everyone who has ever changed careers or been through a divorce or lost a loved one knows something about it. At such times, one feels disoriented and confused, hopeful one moment and despairing the next, a little crazy, very alone and unable to communicate effectively with others."

Other models express differing approaches for understanding change but reflect the grieving framework in the strategies for managing change. Daryl Conner, in his book *Managing at the Speed of Change*, identifies control as the key to understanding change. "Three important implications can be drawn from this model. Change is considered major when it is perceived to be so by those affected. Major change is the result of significant disruption in established expectations. Major change occurs when people believe they have lost control over some important aspect of their lives or their environment." Loss of control is Conner's focus for understanding human reaction to change and the main reason people resist change. "We do not resist the intrusion of something new into our lives as much as we resist the resulting loss of control. In fact, the phrase resistance to change can be considered somewhat misleading. People don't resist change as much as its implications—the ambiguity that results when the familiar ceases to be relevant." In Conner's Structure of Change model, resilience is the key to a successful strategy for managing change. Resilience is defined as "the ability to absorb high levels of change while displaying minimal dysfunctional behavior." The skill, or ability, is defined further through five characteristics demonstrated by resilient people.

**Conner's Five Characteristics of Resilience**

| | |
|---|---|
| 1. Positive | "Display a sense of security and self-assurance that is based on their view of life as complex but filled with opportunity." |
| 2. Focused | "Have a clear vision of what they want to achieve." |
| 3. Flexible | "Demonstrate a special pliability when responding to uncertainty." |
| 4. Organized | "Develop structured approaches to managing ambiguity." |
| 5. Proactive | "Engage change rather than defend against it." |

Although Conner does not provide a clear method or process for building resilience, he provides "an analogy between increasing resilience and the issue of whether creativity is an acquired skill or an inherent trait. In the past, people thought creativity was a gift either you had or you didn't. Most educators now believe that people operate with a baseline capacity for creativity that, if strong enough, can be nurtured and developed into a much more powerful capability." He identifies two types of people, danger-oriented people (type-D) and opportunity-oriented people (type-O), and attributes higher levels of change management success to type-O people who demonstrate his five characteristics of resilience. Although initially Conner's approach does not seem to be built on the grieving framework, his five characteristics strongly reflect the strategies employed by grieving-based models.

Another popular work on change is Erik Olesen's *12 Steps to Mastering the Winds of Change*. In this work Olesen identifies Bridges's model as generally representing the change process. The steps recommended by Olesen for managing change target the emotions and attitudes experienced during Bridges's three phases, and they are positioned as helping individuals take advantage of change as they move through the stages. "Every change, even those that are negative, presents an opportunity. Thus, change can be an all—but only if we know how to take advantage of it." Olesen outlines twelve steps designed to take advantage of change experiences. Eleven of the twelve steps are clearly targeting the cognitive and emotional processes associated with a grieving framework of change. In step ten Olesen targets the physical elements of stress associated with change.

1. View change as a challenge.
2. Learn from mistakes.
3. Build your commitment through goals.
4. Maintain perspective.
5. Maintain passion.
6. Tune the body.
7. Stay committed when the going gets tough.
8. Build self-confidence.
9. Know when to control, when to let go.
10. Communicate effectively.
11. Deal with setbacks and go forward with love.
12. Be optimistic.
13. Use humor.

The Personal Response to Transition model created by Nancy Schlossberg considers individual characteristics along with two additional filters or variables: perception and environment. According to Schlossberg's model, the type of adaptation required to successfully manage change is based upon the combination of variables presented. Adaptation for any transition may be different based on the individual and his or her situation. Four categories—situation, self, supports, and strategies—are applied as criteria for assessing individual strengths and weaknesses. Any area determined to be a weakness is targeted and modified as a method for easing the pain of the transition. Initially, Schlossberg's approach seems to be based on a framework other than the grieving framework. However, all change, whether retirement, job shift, or loss of a loved one is viewed the same, which is similar to all grieving-based models. Schlossberg's approach is similar to

Conner's except Conner would place individual characteristics and perception of the change in the same node.

The approach to understanding change presented by Sabina Spencer and John Adams in their work *Life Changes* captures some of the key elements found in the previous models. Their approach integrates the element of loss (Kubler-Ross), the issues of control and vision (Conner), the elements of endings and beginnings (Bridges), and the element of exploration (Jaffe and Scott). The authors identify a total of seven stages individuals pass through when experiencing change. This approach seems to come closer than the other models to applying a non-grieving-based framework for understanding change. The uniqueness of the model rests in the pit stage that separates the struggle of personal inquiry from the struggles of loss, control, and letting go of the past.

Although this approach breaks the transition process into smaller steps, the explanation of the stages and the recommendations for moving forward are similar to those of grieving-based models. The author's recommendations for managing change include keeping a journal, talking through your feelings, seeking professional counseling, and looking toward the future. "It's now that you must start putting lots of energy into looking toward the future. You don't have to take any big steps, but it helps to give yourself some small successes so that you can begin to move forward." The authors identify the pit stage as the lowest emotional state of the change process. This is also different from the other models, which identify denial and loss as the lowest emotional state.

## SUMMARY

The previous authors and models represent the accepted, contemporary approaches to understanding change. Each approach reflects the grieving framework as the basis for understanding change or at least for dealing with it. Even organizational change models that apply an organizational development perspective of the change process fall back on the grieving process to find strategies for helping people deal with change.

Resistance of change by workers is cited as a main reason change initiatives fail. James O'Toole, author of *Leading Change*, described resistance as puzzling. "It seemed as if everyone was resisting change particularly the people who had to do the most changing. And the most puzzling aspect of this resistance was that people resisted not only bad or harmful change, but also change that was clearly in their own self-interest." The framework we employ for understanding change provides explanation for resistance. The fact that people experience fear, denial, and anger when exposed to imposed change is normal. It is also normal that people should desire to avoid unpleasant situations. However, an important distinction exists between job loss and the loss of a loved one. That distinction is the dimension of grief. Edgar Jackson, in his book *Understanding Grief: Its Roots, Dynamics, and Treatment*, deals with this distinction. "We are not dealing with mild sorrow or mere personal disappointment, though the word 'grief' is sometimes attached to such states. We are thinking of grief as a more specific and intense form of sorrow that is related to the loss by death of one who is dearly loved. It is more than the instinctual loss that might produce important behavioral conditioning in an animal, or even in a young child. It is essentially the emotional and related reactions that occur at the time of and following the loss by death of an important person in the emotional life of an individual who has reached the state of development where he has the capacity for object love."

I believe it is safe to say most Americans do not share the same level of love for their jobs or work assignments as they do for a dear loved one. There may be a small percentage of the workforce that truly love their work and possess the emotional attachment that precipitates grief as defined by Jackson. However, most people do not possess this type of emotional attachment to their work. As Jackson further defines grief he provides additional insight. "The grief feeling has many of the elements of depression but on a temporary basis usually. The main difference is that in grief there is no loss of self-esteem, though there may be a normal amount of self-accusation and feelings of guilt." Studies have shown workers have an identity or self-worth attachment to the job or work they perform. And people in general will protect their self-concept, as explained by Manning and Curtis in their book *Human Behavior: Why People Do What They Do.* "People use defense mechanisms to preserve both biological and emotional health. Biological protection ranges from the large muscle movements that allow you to fight off physical attack to the microscopic efforts of white blood corpuscles that enable you to combat infection and disease. In a healthy person, such biological defenses are natural and automatic reactions to physical threat. In a similar way, you preserve emotional well-being through psychological defense mechanisms. This often subconscious behavior brought into operation to protect feelings of self-worth and a positive self-concept." The experience of job loss or job change that tends to cause denial and feelings of anger are temporary; however, left unattended, they can lead to feelings of inadequacy and hopelessness, coupled with a general sluggishness of thought and behavior that may be attached to a damaged self-esteem. These reactions have traditionally been understood through grief-based models. However, a framework based on behavior style also explains these reactions as well as esteem damage and change resistance. Each behavioral style seeks different meaning in work. If behavioral style needs are being fulfilled in a work environment and that environment is threatened by change, the change will be resisted. If the change is implemented and the style needs continually go unmet, self-esteem issues may arise and the resistance may become stronger.

When a behavioral style framework is applied to understanding the sources of resistance to change, we discover people could resist and struggle with change for reasons other than generalized grief and loss. All change has loss and control issues associated with it, and all change has associated resistance; however, to assume they flow from the same source may be applying a wrong framework of change. Employing a behavioral style-based framework versus a grief-based framework for understanding organizational change may provide different conclusions, which suggests different strategies for managing organizational change. For example: using the Life Orientations (LIFO) behavioral theory as the basis, we note each style has differing needs in work.

Supporting–Giving:      Needs to work hard, prove self-worth, and seek excellence in all they do.

Controlling–Taking:      Needs to get results, prove competence through achievement, and seize opportunities.

Conserving–Holding:      Needs to go slow and think before acting. Wants to make the most of what he or she has by building on what already exists.

Adapting–Dealing:      Needs to please other people in his or her work and maintain harmony in relationships.

When faced with imposed change, the general emotions of denial, anger, and loss will be experienced. Once the emotions are processed, the behavioral source of resistance emerges. The Supporting–Giving individual will resist the change because it may be under his or her ability to perform at high levels while meeting his or her need for excellence. This is a reaction to the lack of clear performance goals, job expectations, and direction that typically exist during times of organizational change. The Controlling–Taking individual will resist change because it may hinder her or his ability to get results and achieve goals. This is a reaction to shifting priorities, unclear goals, and a lack of resources that typically exist during times of organizational change. The Conserving–Holding individual will resist change because it may hinder his or her need for accurate information, detailed planning, and playing it safe. The uncertainty that exists during times of organizational change and the inability to "test" the change prior to implementation can be viewed by this style as risky and unnecessary, which becomes the source of resistance. The Adapting–Dealing style will resist change because of the perceived negative impact on people. The change may hinder her or his ability to meet the needs of others, which leaves her or his needs unmet and tends to create chaos, which is not conducive to harmony.

Because organizational change is typically perceived as imposed change, similar to losing a loved one, the issues of control and loss, and the associated emotions, may be similar; however, that is where the similarities end. The difference lies in resistance. Resistance can be clearly identified when it is seen. The behaviors and emotions associated with resistance are limited and definable. We conclude resistance flows from what is known about the emotions associated with change. Because these are closely associated with the process of grieving, the grieving-based framework for understanding change is reinforced. If these conclusions are wrong it would explain why the strategies recommended for managing change fail and why organizational strategies for overcoming resistance fail. If we change our framework for understanding change, we must automatically adjust the strategies commonly associated with the original framework. The new strategies based on individual behavioral needs may produce different results. The results could be the development of individuals who are truly flexible, adaptable, and open to change in their lives—a workforce that thrives in dynamic changing work environments.

## REFERENCES

Atkins, Stuart. The Name of Your Game. Beverly Hills, CA: Ellis & Stewart Publishers, 1981.

Boyett, Joseph, Boyett, Jimmie. The Guru Guide: The Best Ideas of the Top Management Thinkers. New York, NY: John Wiley & Sons, 1998.

Bridges, William. Transitions: Making Sense of Life's Changes. Reading, MA: Addison-Wesley Publishing, 1980.

Bridges, William. Managing Transitions. Making the Most of Change. Reading, MA: Addison-Wesley Publishing, 1991.

Burke, Kenneth. Permanence and Change: An Anatomy of Purpose. Berkeley, CA: University of California Press, 1954.

Conner, Daryl. Managing at the Speed of Change. New York, NY: Villard Books, 1993.

Conner, Daryl. William Branner, Charles Kiefer, Anthony Carnevale, and Klas Mellander. (1992). "Five Views of Change." Training & Development, March, 34-37.

Hudson, Frederic M. The Adult Years: Mastering the Art of Self-Renewal. San Francisco, CA: Jossey-Bass, 1991.

Jackson, Edgar J. Understanding Grief: Its Roots, Dynamics, and Treatment. Nashville, TN: Abington Press, 1957.

Kubler-Ross, Elisabeth. On Death and Dying. New York, NY: Macmillan, 1969.

Kubler-Ross, Elisabeth. Working it Through. New York, NY: Macmillan, 1982.

Kubler-Ross, Elisabeth. Death: The Final Stage of Growth. Englewood Cliffs, NJ: Prentice-Hall, 1975.

Fulton, Robert. Death and Identity. New York, NY: John Wiley & Sons, 1965.

Goman, Carol K. Adapting to Change: Making it Work for You. Menlo Park, CA: Crisp Publications, 1992.

Manning, George and Curtis, Kent. Human Behavior: Why People Do What They Do. Cincinnati, OH: South-Western Publishing, 1988.

Noer, David M. Healing the Wounds, Overcoming the Trauma of Layoffs and Revitalizing Downsized Organizations. San Francisco, CA: Jossey-Bass, 1993.

Olesen, Erik. 12 Steps to Mastering the Winds of Change. New York, NY: Maxwell Macmillan International, 1993.

O'Toole, James. Leading Change: The Argument for Values-Based Leadership. New York, NY: Ballantine Books, 1996.

Peck, Scott M. The Different Drum: Community Making and Peace. New York, NY: Simon and Schuster, 1987.

Pfeiffer, William. (1991). "Theories and Models in Applied Behavioral Science." 4, Theories and Models, (selected readings).

Pivcevic, Edo. Change and Selves. New York, NY: Oxford Press, 1990.

RIGHT Associates. Dispelling the Myths of Downsizing. Philadelphia, PA: RIGHT Associates, 1992.

Schlossberg, Nancy K. (1987). "Taking the Mystery Out of Change." The Best of Psychology Today, May.

Scott, Cynthia, and Jaffe, Dennis. Managing Change at Work. Menlo Park, CA: Crisp Publications, 1989.

Scott, Cynthia, and Jaffe, Dennis. Managing Personal Change. Menlo Park, CA: Crisp Publications, 1989.

Spencer, Sabina, and Adams, John. Life Changes: Growing Through Personal Transitions. San Luis Obispo, CA: Impact Publishers, 1990.

# Chapter Two

## The Elusive Paragon

## Keith Grant

### INTRODUCTION

Peter M. Senge popularized the concept of a Learning Organization in his book *The Fifth Discipline: The Art and Practice of the Learning Organization*, published in 1990. Since that time, learning has been added to the list of behavioral dimensions examined by organization development practitioners. Organizational learning became a business trend in the 1990s and early Subsequent strategies for creating the Learning Organization included structure, systems, strategic planning, and the application of existing knowledge. Consultants, researchers, and authors scoured the business landscape seeking model organizations that represent the Learning Organization in practice. The results are reflected in numerous books, case studies, and papers published on the topic.

### THE DEFINITION OF A LEARNING ORGANIZATION

In business, healthcare, and academia, there is still debate over the definition of a Learning Organization. Even among sources referred to in this paper, no two sources completely agree on a single definition. Peter Senge defines organizational learning as a "principle or discipline" and the Learning Organization as a "place where people are continually discovering how they create their reality and how what they create can change it." He also distinguishes between people who are educated and people who are *learners*, and the effect this difference has on the organization. This differentiation is critical because Senge's concept of the Learning Organization is based on the individual. "Organizations learn only through individuals who learn. Individual learning does not guarantee organizational learning, but without it no organizational learning occurs." According to Senge, the difference between the educated and learners is personal mastery. Without individuals in the organization who have achieved personal mastery, the organization will not learn.

Calhoun Wick, author of *The Learning Edge*, agrees with Peter Senge on his definition of a Learning Organization, and he also approaches learning from the individual perspective. Wick breaks the Learning Organization down to a formula where "each element of the formula is absolutely mandatory. If one element is missing, your organization will either learn the wrong things or learn at a rate less than its full potential." Wick's formula for a Learning Organization doubles as a guideline for achieving strategic alignment. His formula is:

**Learning Organization = Leader with Vision x (Plan/Metrics) x Information x Inventiveness x Implementation.**

According to Wick, the formula begins with the leader. "Without a leader committed to learning, an organization will never approach its potential for success. Only the leader can commit the organization to facing reality head-on. From his or her vantage point, the leader is the one best positioned to see and articulate the performance gap between what the organization currently achieves and what the organization needs to achieve in the future." This is based on the belief that learning begins with the individual, and again Wick quotes Senge: "Real learning gets to the heart of what it means to be human. Through learning, we recreate ourselves. Through learning, we become able to do something we never were able to do. Through learning, we re-perceive the world and our relationship to it. Through learning, we extend our capacity to create, to be part of the generative process of life."

This strong belief in the individual combined with his belief in the role of the leader makes Wick's formula highly dependent on the organization's leader. If the leader is not leading the organization toward learning, Wick believes learning in the organization will not take place. For Senge, all organizational learning and team learning begin with the individual. For Wick, the individual must be the organization's leader.

According to Wick's formula, only a leader who possesses vision will be effective in developing or creating a learning organization. For his definition of "vision", Wick quotes John Kotter, a professor at Harvard Business School: "What's critical about vision is not its originality, but how well it serves the interests of important constituencies—customers, stockholders, employees—and how easily it can be translated into a realistic competitive strategy. Bad visions tend to ignore the legitimate needs and rights of important constituencies favoring, say employees over customers or stockholders. Or they are strategically unsound. When a company that has never been better than a weak competitor in an industry suddenly starts talking about becoming number one that is a pipe dream, not a vision."

According to Senge, vision is what drives us on a personal level to achieve the apparently unachievable—even to become number one in an industry where currently we may only be a weak competitor. Furthermore, Senge's concept of vision greatly differs from Wick's (and Kotter) in that; according to Senge, "The ability to focus on ultimate intrinsic desires, not only on secondary goals, is a cornerstone of personal mastery. Real vision cannot be understood in isolation form the idea of purpose." It is tied to a deep personal desire of who we are and what we believe we can achieve. In explaining the connection between vision and purpose, Senge quotes George Bernard Shaw. "This is the true joy in life, the being used for a purpose recognized by yourself as mighty one...the being a force of nature instead of a feverish, selfish little clod of ailments and grievances complaining that the world will not devote itself to making you happy."

According to Senge, vision fuels personal mastery, which is the spirit of the learning organization. Once personal mastery is enabled in individuals, learning will take place and flow from within the organization as individuals work together. This approach is very similar to Stephen Covey's concept of personal true north, presented in his book *Seven Habits of Highly Effective People*. Wick, on the other hand, approaches vision from a strategic planning perspective and, therefore, considers vision to be part of a leader's responsibility for creating effective strategic alignment. Effective strategic alignment is required to move the organization to a learning state and to a competitive state within its industry. Here lie the single most significant differences between Wick and Senge. Additional authors examined in our study would agree that leadership plays an important role in formalizing learning in the organization; however, Wick is the only author who lays this responsibility completely at the feet of leadership.

A different perspective of the Learning Organization is provided by Chris Argyris in his book *Organizational Learning: A Theory of Action Perspective*. Argyris defines organizational learning in terms of action theories. "Organizational learning involves the detection and correction of error. When the error detected and corrected permits the organization to carry on its present policies or achieve its present objectives, then that error-detection and correction process is single loop learning. Single-loop learning is like a thermostat that learns when it is too hot or cold and turns the heat on or off. The thermostat can perform this task because it can receive information (the temperature of the room) and take corrective action. Double-loop learning occurs when error is detected and corrected in ways that involve the modification of an organization's underlying norms, policies and objectives."

Argyris's approach to organizational learning is built on theories of action. As an individual becomes familiar with organizational norms, his theory of action will become consistent and predictable against norms or shared organizational maps. When double-loop learning takes place, the individual must adjust his theory of action to align with the organization's new norms or maps.

Karen Watkins and Victoria Marsick, in there work *Sculpting the Learning Organization*, define the Learning Organization as "one that learns continuously transforms itself. Learning takes place in individuals, teams, the organization, and even communities in which the organization interacts. Learning is a continuous, strategically used process, integrated with and running parallel to work. Learning results in changes in knowledge, beliefs, and behaviors." This definition ties change directly to learning. In this approach the organization must invest heavily in the training and empowerment of its people. Empowerment in this case focuses on the freedom and climate that encourages inquiry. Watkins and Marsick refer to this as "inquiry in action." Inquiry is the critical difference between talk, and talk as a medium of learning. The organization must encourage "open-minded curiosity that enables us to suspend our presuppositions and judgments in the interest of the truth or a better solution." Senge defines the learning medium of talk further by defining the differences between discussion and dialogue. According to Senge, dialogue reflects, "deep listening" and discussion reflects stated and defended views. Watkins and Marsick limit the medium of talk to inquiry, probing, and analyzing a topic.

According to Watkins and Marsick, technology and information systems enable people within the organization to put their learning to work. The result is workers with the ability to create "something with nothing" and help determine the very survival of the organization through continuous transformation and growth. The organization improves its capability to respond to change and to do new things effectively. In this approach, an organization either becomes a Learning Organization or eventually ceases to exist.

In contrast to previous authors, Peter Kline and Bernard Saunders define the Learning Organization in their work, *Ten Steps to a Learning Organization,* as "an organization that learns on its own, quite apart from the many individual learnings that will also take place within it. What we envision is an organization whose design takes into account the needs of the people that make them up. Just as physical structures can be designed ergonomically so that the human body can be comfortable with them, the Learning Organization is envisioned as an organization whose structure is fully compatible with human psychology, one which invites joyous affirmation of everything an organization must do to achieve its community-enriching goals." A Learning Organization according to this definition must be aligned with the human psychology of work. Work must never be unrewarding and should be efficient. "The most efficient workers are often also the happiest. While that is not invariably true, it is true that no job and no career need be fundamentally unrewarding. Work that is unrewarding is usually organized in a way that we might call 'brain antagonistic.' That is, it does not fit well with the way the human brain is used to operating." Therefore, in order to become a Learning Organization, all work must align with how humans like to work, and both reward and performance management systems must not cause people to feel unrewarded.

Kline and Saunders have identified sixteen principles that promote learning by creating in a more "brain-compatible" way.

1. Prime every level of the mind of the individual to be self-directed.
2. View mistakes as stepping stones to continuous learning and essential to further business growth.
3. There must be willingness to rework organizational systems and structures of all types.
4. Because learning is an emotional process, the corporate culture must be a supportive place.
5. Celebrate the learning process for it owns sake, not just its end product.
6. Celebrate all learners equally.

7. Accomplish as much transfer knowledge and power from person to person as possible.
8. Encourage and teach learners to structure their own learning, rather than structuring it for them.
9. Teach the process of self-evaluation.
10. Recognize and accept as a goal the complete liberation of all human intelligence everywhere.
11. Recognize that different learning preferences are alternate tools for approaching and accomplishing learning.
12. Encourage people to discover their own *learning* and *thinking styles* and make them accessible to others.
13. Cultivate each employee's abilities in all fields of knowledge and spread the idea that nothing is forever inaccessible to people.
14. Recognize that in order to learn something so it is easy for you to use it, it must be logical, moral, and fun.
15. Ideas can be developed best through dialogue and discussion.
16. Everything is subject to reexamination and investigation.

Kline and Saunders present these sixteen principles as a standard to measure the progress of a developing Learning Organization.

To better understand these principles, Kline and Saunders identify four basic barriers to learning. While the first barrier is more general in nature and the authors do not spend time defining it, the remaining three are referred to as "inner barriers to learning." "Human beings are born with an instinct for learning, which they lose only under duress. We could learn all the time if we were not prevented by one of these barriers."

The first barrier, according to Kline and Saunders, is the *I Can't Barrier*. But once that barrier is broken, the inner three barriers must be broken as well. "When confronted with something that doesn't make sense, we face a *(1) Logical Barrier*. If we're asked to think or do something that by our standards is unethical, we're blocked by a *(2) Ethical Barrier*. And finally, if the process we're involved in makes us uncomfortable, then a *(3) Feeling Barrier* inhibits our learning."

According to the authors, the organization plays a significant role in helping individuals break through the learning barriers. The organization must create a work environment where individuals can become learners and take responsibility for themselves. When this is achieved, the organization can move toward becoming a true Learning Organization. But the greatest incentive to inspire people to reactivate their instinctual capacity to learn comes from the successful experience of learning itself. Therefore, the work environment the organization must create needs to be aligned with the way people work, enabling them to take responsibility, and it needs to provide successful learning experiences for its employees.

## STRATEGIES FOR CREATING LEARNING ORGANIZATIONS

When an organization chooses to become a Learning Organization, it must first agree on a definition. The definition selected is critical, for it helps the process and target of the change for the organization. When it comes to creating a Learning Organization, however, the definition does not always drive the specific strategies needed for achieving the change. It is almost as if learning is a by-product of the change process itself, or a natural result of implementing the selected strategies.

In the book *The Learning Imperative*, Michael Beer, Russell Eisenstat and Bert Spector include a chapter titled "Why Change Programs Don't Produce Change." The chapter deals with why change projects fail, even projects such as a company deciding to become a Learning Organization. They concluded that the goal for this type of change should not be learning but task alignment. In a sense their approach to becoming a Learning Organization is similar to Wick. They identified six strategies for creating a Learning Organization. The strategies are sequential, overlapping steps for developing a "self-reinforcing cycle of commitment, coordination, competence." The authors emphasized the timing and sequence of the steps, which make wonderful sense in the healthcare delivery setting. The following are their six steps:

1. Mobilize commitment to change through *joint diagnosis* of business problems.
2. Develop a *shared vision* of how to organize and manage for competitiveness.
3. Foster *consensus for the new vision*, competence to enact it, and cohesion to move it along.
4. *Spread revitalization* to all departments without pushing it from the top.
5. *Institutionalize revitalization* through formal policies, systems, and structure.
6. *Monitor and adjust strategies* in response to problems in the revitalization process.

According to Beer, Eisenstat, and Spector, learning will take place when change is done correctly in the organization. Successful change can be achieved by applying the above six steps in the appropriate sequence. Each step is based on the people and systems working together to solve business problems to achieve a future condition.

In *Ten Steps to a Learning Organization*, Kline and Saunders lay out their process for becoming a Learning Organization. Again, as each step is implemented, the sixteen principles mentioned earlier will be realized by the organization. Each step is designed to create the type of culture and climate needed for the emergence of a Learning Organization. Their steps are as follows:

1. Assess your learning culture
2. Promote the positive
3. Make the workplace safe for thinking.
4. Reward risk taking
5. Help people become resources for each other.
6. Put learning power to work
7. Map out the vision
8. Bring the vision to life
9. Connect the system
10. Get the show on the road

Beer, Eisenstat, and Spector, and Kline and Saunders agree that vision and getting people involved with the change are important to its overall success. Kline and Saunders add three unique steps to produce organizational learning: assessing your learning culture, helping people become resources for each other, and putting learning power to work. Senge and Watkins also reflect the additional dimension of people working together and consciously focusing on learning as a tool. Learning is positioned as important in the organization and provides the motivation for getting others involved in problem solving. For example, a particular healthcare provider may not have the technical or experiential background to help a group of workers address a particular problem, but may be invited to participate to provide additional perspective on the problem or help the group learn from the problem-solving experience.

In Watkins and Marsick's six steps of action imperative for creating a Learning Organization, the steps are not required to be in any special sequence, because the organization must train heavily and create a culture and work climate that encourage freedom and individual inquiry. Their steps for creating Learning Organizations are as follows:

1.  Create continuous learning opportunities
2.  Promote inquiry and dialogue
3.  Encourage collaboration and team learning
4.  Establish systems to capture and share learning
5.  Empower people toward a collective vision
6.  Connect the organization to its environment

The above steps from Watkins and Marsick are in harmony with the processes proposed by Beer, Eisenstat, and Spector, by Kline and Saunders, by Wick, and by Senge. Except for Wick, all authors agree that the organization requires a vision of the future or a future target for change. All members of the organization must embrace the vision if it is to be reached. Although the authors would disagree about the role vision plays in becoming a Learning Organization, all would agree that it is a critical component.

## CONCLUSION

All of the authors studied in preparation for this paper agreed that the following areas are important to creating a Learning Organization, and we feel that they apply very well to American hospitals:

1. Organizational learning is directly connected to the organization's culture and value system.
2. Organizational learning must be strategically planned, and strategic alignment must be achieved within the organization in order for learning to proliferate.
3. Vision is needed to provide a future context for learning and provide a purpose and target for organizational change.
4. Individuals must communicate with one another. Communication is both a catalyst for learning and a process for multiplying and reinforcing learning.
5. Leadership plays a key role in positioning learning as an organizational norm.

In this chapter, I have sought to shed some light on the factors leading to successful learning in organizations.

## REFERENCES

Argyris, Chris, and Schon, D. 1978. *Organizational Learning: A Theory of Action Perspective.* Menlo Park, CA: Addison-Wesley Publishing.

Howard, Robert, et. Eds. 1990. *The Learning Imperative*. Boston: Harvard Business School. (Selected readings).

Kline, P. and Saunders, B. 1993. *Ten Steps to a Learning Organization.* Arlington, VA: Great Ocean Publisher.

Watkins, K and Marsick, V. 1993. Sculpting the Learning Organization: Lessons in Art and Science Systemic Change. San Francisco, CA: Jossey-Bass Publishers.

Wick, C. 1993. *The Learning Edge*. New York: McGraw-Hill.

# CHAPTER THREE

## LEADERSHIP TAXONOMY

### JEANETTE PACK, DM
### IONIE DOUGLAS, DM
### KEITH GRANT, PhD
### JANIS L. McFAUL, PhD

The purpose of the leadership taxonomy is to provide instructors, students, and practitioners with historical perspectives of the various theories and models around this topic. This taxonomy is not all-inclusive; however, we have outlined over twenty major models and theories on leadership. We have highlighted what we think are some of the major influences in this field. Finally, our goal in this chapter is to offer a high-level view of the complexity and richness of research.

# *Taxonomy of Leadership*

| Theories/ Models Authors | Description of Leadership | Three Major Characteristics | Functions (ROLES, BEHAVIOR, DECISION-MAKING) | Evaluation |
|---|---|---|---|---|
| *The Republic,* Plato, 4th century BC | Leadership is based on law and order. | Influential, popular by consent, or coercive. | The statesman rules with reason and justice; the commander rules with military abilities; and the businessman provides material needs. | Leadership with influence and power are still popular. |
| *The Prince,* Machiavelli, 1513 | Leadership is based on the law and by force. Associated with unethical and coercive leadership. | Strong, ruthless, and cynical for governmental leadership. | Politically-calculated decision-making for control and power. | Present guide for effective leadership and basis for the Mach scale. |
| *Tao Te Ching,* Lao-tsu, 6th century BC | Themes of Eastern philosophy, self-lessness, and nondirective leadership. | Selfless, maintains true self interest, and unbiased leadership. | The role of the facilitator leading the group process. | Advocated for today's leadership. |
| Satyagraha, Gandhi, 1869 | Nonviolence, charismatic, and transformational style. | Resilient, calm, and maintains a sense of humor during crisis. | Motivator, achiever, and support for followers. | Leadership is effective during crisis. |

| | | | | |
|---|---|---|---|---|
| Bureaucratic Leadership, Weber, 1922 | Bureaucracy of order and systems. | Specific areas of responsibility, expert training, and dedication to the job. | High hierarchy structure implementing rules and regulations. | Impersonal and strict rules and regulations. |
| Leadership Styles Theory, Stodgill, 1948 | Autocratic, democratic, and laissez-faire. | Tight control, Participation, and inactive control. | Dictates orders, facilitates, or may have no control. | Defined leadership behavioral style. |
| Trait Leadership Theory, Stodgill, 1948 | Studies of leadership based on traits of personality and character. | Qualities, skills, and characteristics are determined by the situation. | Organizes operative efforts, gains insight into needs of people and the organization. | Leadership requires personal and situational attributes. |
| Maturity–immaturity Theory, Argyris, 1957 | Based on double-loop model of a learning environment. | Self-directed, Motivated, and responsible. | Promotes a learning environment for the creativity of the followers. | The double-loop model is effective for the individual and the organization. |
| Contingency Leadership Theory, Fiedler, 1964 | Based on the task-relations motivated styles. | Task motivator dictates orders, the relations motivator is attentive. | Task-motivator is autocratic; the relations-motivator has participative and considerate manner. | The theory is strongly supported by research studies. |

| Situational Leadership Model, Hersey & Blanchard, 1973 | Based on the task-relations orientation styles. | Tasks or personal relationships, and views job and maturity levels of the followers. | Task-oriented is autocratic, relations-oriented is delegated based on maturity level. | Popular, but under-researched and controversial. |
|---|---|---|---|---|
| Organizational Leadership, McGregor, 1960 | Organizational leadership of Theory X and Theory Y. | The leader must determine if the individual is passive, resistant, or motivated. | Attempts to direct, motivate and develop the group process. | Theory X: more coercive and persuasive. Theory Y: more democratic and person-centered. |
| The Managerial Grid Model, Blake and Mouton, 1964 | Measured leadership by managerial grid for task-relations oriented styles. | Concerned about employees and work, concerned about employees only, or goal-centered. | Task-oriented is autocratic, relation seeks participation and decision with teams. | 9.9 style popular with teams for 20th century U.S. presidents. |
| Eupsychian Management Model, Maslow, 1965 | Developing self-esteem, psychological health, and self-actualization of subordinates. | Democratic superior, spontaneously democratic or based on the situation. | Support person, motivator, give praise and feedback. | Leadership is given to individuals best suited for the situation. |
| Multi-Linkage Model, Yukl, 1971 | Leader-follower relationship interaction process. | Believes in group cohesiveness, enhanced leadership role, and initiated structure. | Facilitates task completion and enhances follower's effort. | Leadership is effective if the follower is amenable to the interaction process. |

| | | | | |
|---|---|---|---|---|
| Transformational Leadership Theory, Bass, 1985a/b | Charismatic, inspirational, intellectual consideration, and individualized consideration. | Converts followers into leaders, self-confident, and determined. | Uses intellectual and stimulating ways to communicate and motivate. | Driving force in leadership thought and practice. |
| Women as Managers, Grant, 1988 | Based on six psychological qualities. | Qualities, experiences, and opinions of other women leaders are strengths. | As a communicator, autonomous and participatory leader. | No differences emerge between male and female managers. |
| Creative Leadership, Rickard, 1988 | Creative leadership and its application. | Facilitating or process-oriented style, on managing people. | Creativity sessions and brainstorming. | Develops liberating leadership attitude in the wider context. |
| Post-Entrepreneurial Hero, Moss Kanter, 1989 | Based on seven managerial skills and individuals skills. | Self-belief, collaborates with others, and a willingness to learn. | Produces leaders who are result-oriented, entrepreneurial-inclined, and dedicated. | Prospective leader attuned to the realities of the workplace. |
| International Leader, Hogg & Syrett, 1991 | Global leadership. | Diverse experiences, problem-solver, and resilient. | Fluent in language and excellent with diverse groups. | Consistent global exposure is necessary for the international leader. |
| Organization Culture & Leadership, Schein, 1992 | Based on culture within the organization. | Shared values, communicator, and creative. | Communicates with others and works with group. | Cultural understanding is essential for leaders. |

| | | | | |
|---|---|---|---|---|
| The Fifth Discipline Theory, Senge, 1994 | Organizational learning and System Theory. | Create new systems, work collaboratively with others, and learn by doing. | Build shared vision mental models and integration through system thinking. | Organizational learning can be applied to communities. |
| Boccialetti, G. 1995 | Three styles of management: accommodating, autonomous, and adversarial. | Manage yourself when working with authority. | Manager has nine potential styles based on author's research. | Knowledge of styles can improve organizational relations of all employees. |
| In Search of Excellence, Peters & Waterman, Jr., 1996 | Eight attributes for excellence in management. | Vision, persistence, and willingness to take risk. | Do it, fix it, and try it approach to new and old ideas. | Excellent in management takes perseverance, time, and repetition. |
| Learning to Lead, Bennis and Goldsmith, 1997 | The role of future leaders. | Trust, vision, and meaning. | Create a personal agenda for leading. | Empowerment leads to quality and love of self, work, and life. |
| Leadership for the 21st Century, Rost, 1998 | Based on the leader-follower criteria. Leaders have high morals. Ethics are a part of leadership. | Reciprocal role with follower, serve rather than lead, and entrusted individual. | Works with followers to achieve goals and participates in the group process. | Leaders must deal honestly with followers and have a sense of balance in their lives. |

| | | | | |
|---|---|---|---|---|
| Collaborative Leadership, Chrislip & Larson, 1994, 1995* | Based on group process and output. Peers are viewed as equal. | Servant, trans-formative facili-tative model, relationship among persons is reciprocal, nonhierarchical. | Role of facilitator focuses on the collab-orative pro-cess. Trust building is imperative. | Leadership effective for team processes, high degree of col-laboration needed. Extensive research with com-munities. |
| Transforma-tional Leader-ship with the Full Range of Leadership (FRL) model, Bass & Alvo-lio, 1998* | Continuum Model incor-porates transactional and trans-formational behaviors. Laissez-faire = nontransac-tion. | Full sprectrum of leadership behaviors. How leaders help followers cope with organization cultures. | Based on transform & transaction leadership. Laissez-faire, delayed action, ignored responsibili-ties. | Model has high utility for research and practice. |
| Drucker, 1999* | Criteria for "effectiveness," one can be effective with a variety of per-sonality traits. | Executive's job is to be effective. | Effective-ness can be learned. Task: mul-tiply perfor-mance capa-bilities of the whole. | Based on Drucker's experience in man-agement. Leadership and man-agement used inter-changeably. |
| Blank, 2000* | Nine Laws of Leadership, nomenclature: "Quantum Leadership." Influential, popular by consent, or coercive. | Newton's theory is outdated. Reality is a field. Concepts related to "sys-tems." Followers and leaders are willing allies. | Conscious-ness = how informa-tion is processed— creates leadership. Paradigm shift based on natural laws and systems. | Evolving view of leadership that includes followers in the leadership process. |

After reviewing all of the leadership theories and models that are included in the preceding section, what is startling to me is that so many of these "styles" are still being used. You might say, *we haven't evolved much*, but, then again, you might say, *if it isn't broke, then don't fix it!* In modern organizations, we know that there are great leaders and that there are still unbelievably inept leaders that are driving their organizations into extinction (reference Enron).

The key aspect of the preceding chart is to review our evaluation. In his book, *If Aristotle Ran General Motors: The New Soul of Business*, Tom Morris cites that the writings of Plato (428–348 BC) had so much influence on "Western thought ... that Harvard philosopher and mathematician Alfred North Whitehead would, in our century, describe the whole history of philosophy as just a series of footnotes to Plato."

EVERY person in a company needs to act like a leader; EVERY person in the organization needs to be trained on how important the customer is to the overall company. In his 1994 book, *The Customer Comes Second and Other Secrets of Exceptional Service*, **Hal** Rosenbluth talks about the important role that an employee can play in a customer's overall experience. His theory was based on the idea that if an employee is treated well by the company, the customer ultimately will benefit. I believe Rosenbluth was on to something, but, moreover, the gist of his message was that a happy customer equals a successful business. Now that is good leadership!

## RESPONSIBLE LEADERSHIP

What makes a good leader? Who do you look up to? In September 2001, we looked at a young, inexperienced president that was learning his way through a tragedy President George W. Bush, Jr., seemed to grow into his leadership over the next few months. In another part of the United States, Mayor Rudolph Giuliani impressed millions in the United States and worldwide with his composure, compassion, and control over a city that was in shock. (Was that a bit like Gandhi—*a leadership style that is effective during a crisis?*) In an interview in October on CNNs Larry King,

Mayor Giuliani was asked, "What makes you the kind of leader that you are? You are known for bringing calm into times of chaos and chaos in times of calm." Rudy smiled and said that he thought that was probably accurate. And I think that is what great leaders do!

Great leaders take quiet times and say "we can do better," they churn things up and ask 'why not?' But when there is chaos, we look to our leaders for the answers. We need calm. We need reassurance. Giuliani delivered that for not only New Yorkers, but also all Americans. In fact, in the November 19, 2001, issue of Time Magazine they said, "Rudolph Giuliani, the straight-shooting mayor of New York City, often irritated his constituents—with laws governing the "quality of life" and artistic "decency"—but he has proved a paragon of leadership since Sept.11, and last week was able to anoint a successor, media billionaire Michael Bloomberg" (Key Figures, p. 21).

## PREDICTABILITY IN LEADERSHIP STYLE

Knowing what kind of leader you are working for is important. Have you ever dealt with a person that was "moody" or "unpredictable?" You don't know what to expect. Consistency in behavior is important.

In Ken Blanchard's book, *The Heart of Leadership*, he stated that "consistency does not mean behaving the same way all the time. It actually means behaving the same way under similar circumstances." He went on to say that "many leaders make the mistake of letting their moods determine how they respond to their people. When you respond to your people in the same way under similar circumstances, you give them a valuable gift—the gift of predictability."

## REPREHENSIBLE LEADERSHIP

Reprehensible leaders throughout history that come to mind include Hitler, Stalin, Mussolini, and more recently, Osama Bin Laden. One may wonder, if these characters that have changed world history are so reprehensible, then why did people follow them? This chapter is not a history lesson. The holy wars and the ancient feuds are always difficult to understand for those not emotionally connected. Where there is hatred and passionate disagreement—reprehensible leaders can emerge.

But reprehensible leaders can emerge in business, too. The contemporary models are out there for us to study. What happened at Enron, Firestone, all of the dot-coms? History will write those chapters with, perhaps, better perspective than we might have today. And many of those chapters will be written with the help of our courts.

## FINALLY, HOW DO WE TRAIN FUTURE LEADERS?

It is imperative that top leaders within an organization demonstrate what they feel is important. We are all hungry for leadership. We are hungry for guidance. I believe that, for most of us, when we arrive at work we want to contribute. American corporations could have a competitive advantage that we export. Let's get it together.

In our work environment we have all witnessed examples of responsible leadership and reprehensible leadership. How do we train our future leaders? *Well one way might be to review history!*


## *PARTING QUOTES FOR THE TAXONOMY OF LEADERS:*

Some wisdom must be learned
from one who is wise.

—Euripides

A happy life consists in
tranquility of mind.

—Cicero

Those who know the truth are not
equal to those who love it, and
they who love it are not equal to
those who delight in it.

—Confucius

Only the educated are free.                              —Epictetus

What it lies in our power to do, it
also lies in our power not to do.                        —Aristotle

All that we do is done with an eye
to something else.                                       —Aristotle

A horse never runs so fast as
when he has other horses to
catch up and outpace.                                    —Ovid

When all think alike, then no one
is thinking.                                             —Walter Lippman

Every calling is great when
greatly pursued.                            —Oliver Wendell Holmes, Jr

It seems to me that our value
system and world view should be
as closely integrated into our work
lives as they are integrated into
our lives with our families, our
churches, and our other activities
and groups.                                              —Max DePree

There is more to life than
increasing its speed.                            —Mahatma Gandhi

## REFERENCES

Bass, B.M. 1990. *Bass & Stogdill's handbook of leadership: Theory, research and managerial applications (3rd ed.).* New York: The Free Press.

Bennis, W. & Goldsmith, J. 1997. *Learning to lead: A workbook on becoming a leader* (Updated ed.). Reading, Massachusetts: Persus Books.

Dreher, D. 1990. *The Tao of inner peace.* New York: Harper-Collins.

Hackman, M.Z. & Johnson, C.E. 1996. *Leadership: A Communication perspective (2nd ed).* Prospect Heights Illinois: Waveland Press.

Senge, P. 1986. Systems principles for leadership. In (J.D. Adams Ed.).

*Transforming leadership.* Virginia: Miles River Press

Syrett, M. & Hogg, C. (Eds.) 1994. *Frontiers of leadership: An essential reader.*

Great Britain: T.J. Press Ltd.

Wren, T.J. (Ed.) 1995. The *leader's companion: Insights on leadership through the ages.* New York: Simon & Schuster.

Blackwell, Roger, and Stephen, K. 2001. *Customer Rule!: Why the E-Commerce Honeymoon is over and Where Winning Businesses Go from Here.* Crown Publishing.

Blanchard, Ken 1999. *The Heart of a Leader: Insights on the Art of Influence.* Tulsa, Oklahoma, Honor Books.

Morris, Tom 1997. *If Aristotle Ran General Motors: The New Soul of Business.* New York, New York. Henry Holt and Company, Inc. Publishers.

Rayport, J. (July 6, 2000). *Old Rules for a New Economy,* URL: http://ww.zdnet.com/ecommerce/stories/main/0,10475,2599298,00.html

Rosenbluth, Hal F., and McFerrin Peters, D. 1994. *The Customer Comes Second and Other Secrets of Exceptional Service.* Quill Publishing.

# Chapter Four

Things I Learned ... Begin in Organization

Janis McFaul, PhD

These are the life lessons I learned about organizational living. Living the organizational life starts at birth and continues even in death.

The cream does not always rise to the top.

Coffee klatsches can be beneficial to your organization— **listen**, you may learn something!

**W**hat goes around, comes around.
Smart companies listen to their inner compass—the
employees!

**H**istory will repeat itself if we don't pay attention!

Every department is important.  A company, like a family, needs all voices at the dinner table.

Every change agent faces resistance. There are always those who resist change—not because it isn't helpful, but only because it is different.

Every day, in every way, there is beauty around us—even at our work. LOOK FOR IT!

As Confucius said,
*"Everything has its beauty, but not everyone sees it."*

Some companies say that
*"customers are our most important asset."*
But they forget that without their employees they
would not have any customers.
Employees are a company's most important asset.
*Act like it!*

Companies don't really go to school.
But in a way, they do!
Listen to your customers and to your employees.
Remember, *a complaint is a gift*.
It means that your customers or employees care
enough to tell you that they WANT you to change.
Listen!

To be a manager today is one of the hardest jobs out there.  You need to be part teacher, part counselor, and part judge.

Let's not forget the human part...
*the most important part of all!*

$A$ few years ago, Jack Welch said to his staff, for any future promotions or hires you have to explain to me *why*, if your candidate is not a woman or a minority. If more executives acted like Jack, then the top of our corporations would look more like our population. *Accolades to Jack.*

Intel's Andy Grove encouraged all of his employees to spend 10 percent of each workweek contributing to the community.
Can you imagine what the world would be like if every company would encourage employees to volunteer for four hours each week at a nursing home, the Humane Society, the Red Cross, the Salvation Army, or any other good cause?
*I want to live in that world!*

No man is an island.
Nor should an officer of a company act like he or she
alone has all the answers.


Don't be a "knower," be a "learner."
There is no person (leader) who knows everything!
Humble yourself, and learn something new.

Every task is important and should
be done proudly, as long as it is
done with 110% effort.

# 110%

**For global companies, what is stronger?
Our company culture
or
our individual ethnic culture?
Both play an important
role in our doing business
internationally!**

**Groupthink can be dangerous.
As Walter Lippman stated,
"When all think alike, then
no one is thinking!"**

Change is like transplanting a tree.
For many years the tree has stood just
where it is, proud and able to fend for itself.
But now a highway project is going to pass
directly over the tree's location.  The tree can
stand where it is and be bulldozed during the
careless destruction that will accompany the
project.  Or it can be transplanted, to become
the centerpiece of a wonderful garden.

**Diversity
is a key to any successful
organization.** Do our customers all look
alike?
**NO!**
*It is important that our
workforce reflects our
customer base!*

*It is not right to send all of our headquarters personnel to have the key jobs in our overseas offices.*

*Conversely, we must have some representation from the home office and other corporate global sites. Our offices worldwide should be a <u>mosaic</u> of our global workforce.*

Even though our mission statement may say
all the politically correct words,
words are only words until our managers
turn them into deeds!

# Communicate, communicate, and then—just to make sure—communicate once more. Communication is EVERYTHING!

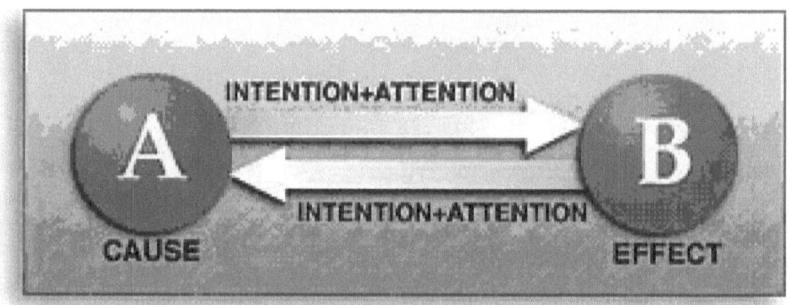

There is a Japanese saying that roughly translates into, "everyone has one blessing." When looking at your staff, remember that.

The 19th century management style:
**The Voice of the Executive**
The 20th century management style:
**The Voice of the Customer**
The 21st century management style:
**The Voice of the Employee**

Start to listen. You don't have to hire a research company: Your focus group is already on site and on your payroll!

# CHAPTER FIVE

## THINGS I LEARNED ...

## KEITH GRANT

I have been in the field of business and education for over thirty years. I have held various positions in different organizations. Although most of my professional development took place in the automotive industry, I learned valuable lessons from other job experiences as well.

### SMALL BUSINESS EXPERIENCE

My first regular working experience was starting my own real estate company with two other partners when I was 18 years old. I had that business for ten years. This experience taught me the finer details of running a small business.

A few key lessons:

- There are many aspects of business, and broad experience is required for success.
- Honesty and integrity are effective business practices.
- We are living the life we choose.

*What are your observations?*

------------------------------------------------
------------------------------------------------
------------------------------------------------
------------------------------------------------
------------------------------------------------
------------------------------------------------

## TEACHING AT A WOMEN'S PRISON

I worked as a college instructor at a women's prison for two years. This job was challenging in positive ways and provided opportunity for personal learning. The experience gave me a sense of importance for treating people as individuals. Theodore White once said, "One sees things for the first time only once." I realized a prisoner was sometimes in the mind of the beholder. This experience sparked a desire within me to learn and to help others achieve their best.

A few key lessons:

- Prisoners and handicapped individuals are people too, with hopes, dreams, skills, and abilities.
- People can be limited by what they believe or don't believe—and so can organizations.
- Don't take your full-functioning facilities for granted.
- Pure verbal communication is difficult. Meaning is in words and tone.
- Change can be a lifelong struggle—against social odds.
- People adapt differently to overcome change barriers.
- Personal change requires various levels of intensity associated with the process.

*What are your observations?*

------------------------------------------------
------------------------------------------------
------------------------------------------------
------------------------------------------------
------------------------------------------------
------------------------------------------------

## FIRST CORPORATE EXPERIENCE

While working and going to college, one job that deserves mentioning was my first job in a corporate environment.

A few lessons:

- Every job is important, even the ones we don't see.
- Procedures, even seemingly simple ones, are usually required for good reasons.
- Most employees don't know the reasons for the procedures they follow.
- Every Chief Executive Officer should work the lowest paid job in their organization for one week a year.
- Diverse job experiences enhance the development process.

### *What are your observations?*

_____
_____
_____
_____
_____
_____

### Automotive Industry Experience

These are my initial memories of my first years working at a large corporation.

A few lessons:

- The importance of procedures and double-blind checking systems.
- The importance of documenting any process.
- A willingness to learn and quality work are usually rewarded.
- When you do something well, you are usually rewarded by getting to do more of it.
- Although many of the dynamics are the same, large corporations are different from smaller businesses.
- Communication between operation shifts must take place at some organizational level.

- To most people, the concept of working together is a win–lose process.

### *What are your observations?*

------------------------------------------------

------------------------------------------------

------------------------------------------------

------------------------------------------------

------------------------------------------------

------------------------------------------------

## Management Experience

As a supervisor, my interest in and exposure to training and education began. I was responsible for seven employees; the environment became a testing ground for the management concepts learned in the classroom. A clash of value, work, and meaning began that will hopefully last a lifetime.

A few lessons:

- The title of manager isn't required to be a good manager.
- Mentoring is a critical process for upward movement in organizations.
- Know your people, and demonstrate care and encouragement.
- Learn as much as possible about your operation and its purpose.
- Change tends to be a control issue with most people.
- Training and knowledge are powerful business tools.

### *What are your observations?*

------------------------------------------------

------------------------------------------------

------------------------------------------------

------------------------------------------------

------------------------------------------------

------------------------------------------------

## EXPANDED BUSINESS EXPERIENCE

The book *Essentials of Management* states, "Managing as practice is art; the organized knowledge underlying it may be referred to as a science. Consequently, science and art are mutually exclusive but are complementary" (Koontz, O'Donnell, and Weikrich, p.7). The field of management has always attracted individuals seeking challenges of leadership, responsibility, and decision-making. During this experience I began to learn the real challenge of leadership: balancing the art with the science.

A few key lessons:

- Financial understanding of the business is critical to decision making and success. Equally critical is understanding people.
- Politics are a reality in any organization, regardless of size or function.
- Politics are an aspect of the organizational climate and one of its determinants. Management behavior is key.
- Employee motivation and performance can be increased and must be managed.
- Managers don't like dealing with "people problems" because they don't know how.
- Leadership is a personal responsibility. It is learned and earned.
- Title and position don't necessarily mean qualified.

### *What are your observations?*

---------------------------------------------------------------
---------------------------------------------------------------
---------------------------------------------------------------
---------------------------------------------------------------
---------------------------------------------------------------
---------------------------------------------------------------

## TRAINING EXPERIENCE

When asked to take on a training position, I was unsure what it would require.

Robert F. Mager said in his book, *Making Instruction Work*, "Just as an ability to make a tuba is not the same as an ability to play one, an ability to play one is not the same as an ability to teach someone else to do likewise. Therefore, those who would like to share their competence with others will take steps to learn the skills by which that end is accomplished." I began seeking formal training in adult learning, communications, and technical training methodologies.

A few key lessons:

- If skill and knowledge are powerful, then learning is more powerful.
- The more you know about the different departments within a company, the clearer the "big picture" becomes.
- A good design may have one application but many opportunities.
- Most of the problems with organizations lie with management.
- There is more to adult learning and instructional design than a few courses.
- People learn in different ways—provide alternative learning methods for the same material.
- Be creative—think out of the box—good things will happen.
- Do the right thing for the people and the organization, even if it hurts.
- Old dogs can learn new tricks  if the old dog wants to learn.
- Success means different things to different people.
- Service is not a tool; it is a belief, a way of life.

### *What are your observations?*

_____

_____

_____

_____

_____

_____

A few lessons:

- The skills of controlling, planning, and organizing are the basics.
- Middle management usually functions in a crisis mode, demonstrating the ability to think and act tactically; however, anticipation, innovation, and strategic thinking provide the greatest organizational impact.
- There are those people who make things happen, those who watch things happen, and those who wonder what happened.
- What we do today affects the future. In fact, it creates it.
- No one can understand organizational direction without management providing a clear, purposeful communication of the "big picture."
- Most managers can't articulate the "big picture."
- Most managers don't understand why people don't do what they want them to do.

### *What are your observations?*

_____

_____

_____

_____

_____

_____

## WORKING WITH EXTERNAL CONSULTANTS

Having worked with external consultants during a management transition, I learned insightful lessons. Our purpose was to increase the effectiveness of the design management.

A few lessons:

- Job changes are excellent development experiences.
- A high performing team of individuals can achieve almost anything.

- People want to own the process and be involved, even if it's painful.
- Organizations develop in specific, measurable ways.
- Measurable and behaviorally stated the goals = easier design.
- Management struggles with change—especially the sharing of authority.
- With every pair of hands hired, a brain comes free.
- Paradigms cause people to define the new in a context of the old.
- Change planning should start with defining the future, the vision, and the ideal. It should not start from the known present.

### What are your observations?

_____
_____
_____
_____
_____
_____

- A model of some kind must be used. The Open Systems model works well when working in a complex organizational problem.
- When working in organization development, never forget that employees are people, not assets.
- Effective organization development programs must start by educating management.
- Effective management development is balanced between organization needs and individual career goals.
- Management behavior plays a major role in the organization's values and climate.
- When paradigms shift, everyone goes back to zero.
- Paradigm paralysis causes people to see changes as threat.

### What are your observations?

_____
_____
_____

---------------------------------------------------------------
---------------------------------------------------------------
---------------------------------------------------------------

## CONSULTING EXPERIENCE

My clients assigned were the following functions: planning, logistics, quality, purchasing, and one assembly plant. This is the job I truly enjoyed the most.

A few key lessons

- Successful internal consulting requires an attitude of customer service.
- Effective consulting requires partnerships and buying in to each other's success.
- It is easy for a consultant to become a pair of hands for the client.
- Quality is more than a program or slogan; it's a belief of the heart.
- Every organization struggles to gain and maintain alignment with core values, ethics, and principles.
- People will not remember how fast you accomplished something, but they will remember the quality with which it was completed.
- The education system can learn from private business, and private business can learn from the education system.
- Sound leadership techniques work, regardless of the work group.
- A successful partnership between business and education can be achieved.
- Accelerated learning techniques truly condense learning times.
- For success, management must address the human side of mergers.
- Both organizations and individuals go through clear, identifiable stages of change.
- Changes cause trust gaps. These gaps can and must be managed during transitions.

- Understanding human relations is essential to understanding organizations.
- Personal development practitioners and change agents should never stop learning.
- Self-empowerment starts with self-awareness and right perspective.
- Without active learning, organizations, like people, will repeat their failures.

### *What are your observations?*

---------------------------------------------------------------
---------------------------------------------------------------
---------------------------------------------------------------
---------------------------------------------------------------
---------------------------------------------------------------
---------------------------------------------------------------

# CHAPTER SIX

## MANAGEMENT TOOLS

## KEITH GRANT

The primary role of management is to plan, organize, lead, and control employees. These activities can only be accomplished by working with and through people (Certo, 1997). Based on this definition for management, this chapter is dedicated to assist you in achieving that role. The chapter is divided into two sections: meeting participants and reviews of various types of quality improvements tools.

### NINE COMMON MEETING PROBLEMS AND THE MEETING FORMULA

1. Floundering
2. Overbearing Participant(s)
3. Dominating Participant(s)
4. Reluctant Participant(s)
5. Unquestioned Acceptance of Opinions as Facts
6. Rush to Accomplishment
7. Wanderlust: Digression and Tangents
8. Feuding Members
9. Late Starters

## 1. Floundering

Floundering Groups commonly have trouble starting and ending a meeting or a project. They wonder what action to take next. Problems getting the meeting started may indicate the group is unclear in its purpose, overwhelmed by its task, not comfortable with one another, unsure of procedures or processes, or lacking strong leadership.

*Suggestions for Overcoming Floundering*

- Get the group to look critically at how the meeting is going.
- Review the purpose of the meeting, and suggest a process for moving forward.
- Review the meeting ground rules and ask for reasons why it is floundering.
- Suggest the problem that is causing the floundering be written as a "parking lot" issue, and move on with the original purpose of the meeting

## 2. Overbearing Participants

Some members wield a disproportionate amount of influence in a meeting. These people usually have a position of authority or an area of expertise on which they base their authority. Many times, groups require an authority or expert to achieve their purpose, and the group benefits from an authority's participation. But the presence of an authority or expert is detrimental when the person:

- Discourages or forbids discussion encroaching into his or her authority or expertise.
- Signals the untouchability of an area by using technical jargon or referring to present specifications, standards, policies, or regulations as the ultimate determinants of the future actions.
- Regularly discounts any proposed activity by declaring that it won't work, isn't needed, or has been unsuccessfully attempted in the past.

These actions soon give members the message that their suggestions or input will be seen as trite or naïve, and they reduce the effectiveness that the meeting will achieve its purpose.

*Suggestions for Overcoming Overbearing Participants*

- Reinforce agreement that no area is sacred in relation to the meeting or problem being addressed.
- Get the authority or expert to agree (before the meeting) that it is important for the group to make its own way and for all members to have input and be heard.
- Talk with the authority or expert in private and ask for their cooperation and patience.
- Enforce the ground rules, and encourage diverse points of view.

## 3. Dominating Participants

Some members, with or without authority or expertise, consume a disproportionate amount of air time. They talk too much. Instead of concise statements, they tell overloaded anecdotes and dominate the meeting. There is no room for silence that can be used for reflection or thought. Their talk inhibits the group from building a sense of accomplishment or momentum. Others may feel discouraged or that the meeting is a waste of time.

*Suggestions for Overcoming Dominating Participants*

- Structure discussion on key issues to encourage equal participation.
- Use techniques such as the affinity process to limit and focus discussion.
- Assign time to each member for input during a round robin process.
- Establish "balance of participation" as a ground rule and/or one of the criteria for evaluating the meeting.
- Assign the role of gatekeeper or facilitator for the meeting.

## 4.     Reluctant Participants

Many meetings have participants who rarely speak, in general, because they are introverted.  They are the opposite of the dominators, who tend to be extroverts.  Each of us has a different threshold of need to be part of a group, and we have different levels of comfort when speaking in front of others (especially work peers).  There is nothing right or wrong about extroverted or introverted individuals; these are just differences between people.  Problems may develop when there are no activities that encourage the introverts to participate and the extroverts to listen.

*Suggestions for Overcoming Reluctant Participants*

•   Structure the meeting the same way as for dominating participants.
•   Structure discussion on key issues to encourage equal participation.
•   Use techniques such as the affinity process to limit and focus discussion.
•   Assign time to each member for input during a round robin process.
•   Establish "balance of participation" as a ground rule and/or one of the criteria for evaluating the meeting.
•   Assign the role of gatekeeper or facilitator for the meeting.

## 5. Unquestioned Acceptance of Opinions as Facts

Some meeting members express personal beliefs and assumptions with such confidence that listeners assume they are hearing facts.  This can be dangerous, leading to an unshakable acceptance of various "earth is flat" assertions.  Many meeting members are reluctant to question statements from self-assured members.  Besides not wanting to be impolite, members think they need data before challenging someone else's assertions.  There is an ancient axiom about debate that says, if a speaker presents something as fact without legitimate supporting evidence, the listener need not have evidence to respond with skepticism.

*Suggestions for Overcoming Unquestioned Acceptance of Opinions as Facts*

- The facilitators can politely ask:
  "Is what you said an opinion or a fact?"
  "How do you know that what you have just said is true?"
  "What supporting data do you have for that conclusion?"
  "Let's deal with known facts at this time."
- Place the information in a "parking lot" to be considered after the process is complete.
- Assign someone in the group to track down the information after the meeting and report back to the group during the next meeting.

## 6. Rush to Accomplishment

Many meetings have at least one member who is either impatient or sensitive to the pressure of accomplishment. This person typically reaches an individual decision about a problem and its solution before the group has had time to consider different options. He or she urges the group to hasty decisions and discourages any further efforts to analyze or discuss the matter beyond his or her conclusion. His or her direct statements and nonverbal behavior communicate impatience. Too much of this pressure can lead a group in quick, unsystematic efforts to solutions and "fix its." Good solutions and improvements rarely come easily. Quality takes patience and time.

*Suggestions for Overcoming Rush to Accomplishment*

- Remind the group of the purpose of the meeting and the agreed upon process or model.
- If you are serving as the facilitator, make certain you are not pressuring participants to rush to accomplishment.
- Confront the rusher by using the technique for constructive feedback, and by helping the person to become aware of his or her actions and how they may impact the results of the meeting.

## 7. Wanderlust: Digression and Tangents

Wide-ranging, unfocused conversations are an example of wanderlust, our natural tendency to stray from the subject. Sometimes these digressions are innocent tangents from the discussion or harmless side conversations. But they also happen when a participant wants to avoid a subject. In either case, the meeting facilitator is responsible for bringing the conversation back to the meeting agenda.

*Suggestions for Overcoming Wanderlust: Digression and Tangents*

- Use a written agenda with time estimates for each item. Refer to the topic and its allocated time when the discussion strays too far. This is usually the responsibility of the assigned gatekeeper or facilitator.
- Write agenda topics and their associated points of discussion on a flip chart as they are addressed. These are posted on the wall where participants can refer to them. These can be used to focus discussion back to the agenda.
- Direct the conversation back on track by saying:
  "We've strayed from the topic, which was_____."
  "The last few comments before we digressed were _____."
  "We are having trouble sticking to the topic. Is there something about it that makes it so easy to get off track?"

## 8. Feuding Members

Sometimes a meeting becomes a field of combat between two or more participants. Other members feel like spectators at a sporting match and fear that, if they participate in any disagreement between the combatants, they will be swept into the contest. Usually these feuds predate the meeting and, in all likelihood, will outlast it, too. The best way to deal with this situation is to prevent it by carefully selecting meeting participants so that adversaries are not in the same meeting. If that is not possible, then bring the combatants together prior to the meeting to work out some agreement about their behavior.

*Suggestions for Overcoming Feuding Members*

- When confrontations occur, capture the issue, and place it in the "parking lot" to be addressed at a later time.
- In the meeting ground rules address the potential behavior. This provides a standard of behavior to safely reference should a confrontation occur.
- Assign one of the combatants the role of gatekeeper. It becomes their job to keep the meeting on track.

## 9. Late Starters

Many organizations suffer from starting every meeting late, no matter its importance, because their cultural norms support this behavior. This can cause members to see the subject or task as unimportant or to reflect poorly on the meeting leader. Even if the problem is company wide, a separate standard can be set for individual meetings. This can be accomplished in a number of ways.

*Suggestions for Overcoming Late Starters*

- Include in the meeting agenda distributed to everyone prior to the meeting that the meeting will start promptly at a particular time. No matter what, begin the meeting at that time.
- Include in the meeting agenda that a fine will be levied on any member who is late. Make the fine fun and unthreatening. Some organizations charge a one dollar fine from each late member. At the end of the month or quarter, the money is donated to a local charity. Whatever is attempted, remember, changing this type of behavior in a company takes time. You can run your meeting in such a way that you gain a reputation for starting your meetings on time and for being punctual at other meetings.

## Meeting Decision Formula

Answer the following questions:

1. Is there a problem to solve or a decision to make that requires input or commitment from others?
2. Is there information needed that others have, or are others needed for information or idea generation?
3. Is there planning or action that requires input or commitment from others?
4. Is there planning or learning to share?
5. Is there any other way of achieving the desired outcome or result?
6. Is there time to hold this meeting?
7. Is this meeting a good use of others' time and company dollars?

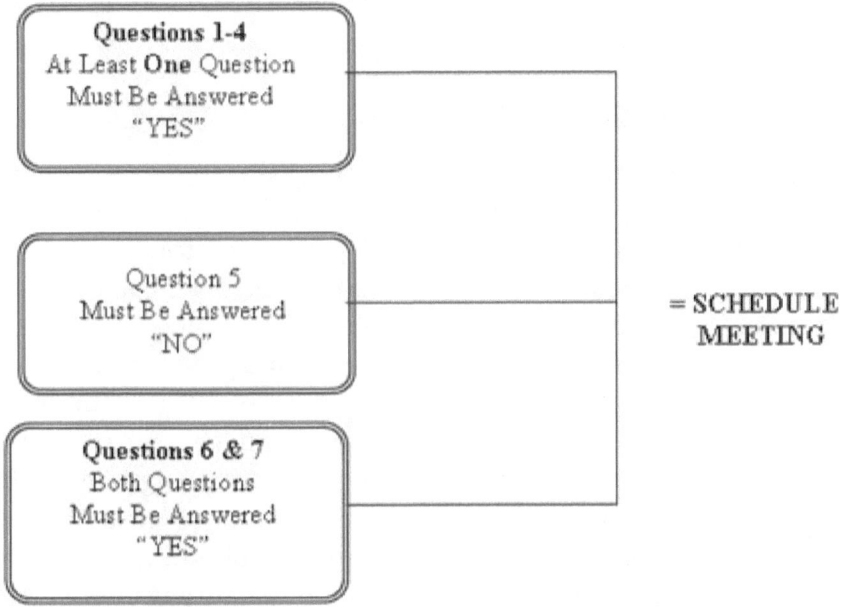

## Meeting Preparation

Meeting Preparation Checklist

1. Is the purpose for the meeting clear?
2. you defined the desired outcomes?
3. Have you challenged the meeting against the Meeting Decision Formula?
4. Is a meeting the best way to achieve the desired outcomes?
5. What type of meeting is it going to be?
6. What process, model, or techniques are you going to use?
7. Is there prework for the meeting?
8. Are all the key people invited?
9. Is there anyone who doesn't really have to be there?
10. How long is the meeting going to be? Is it enough time to achieve the desired outcomes?
11. What equipment or materials are needed?
12. Is the location and time of meeting ideal for the topic?
13. Have you analyzed the audience?
14. Is the agenda clear, and will participants be prepared?
15. What roles will you use? Who will you assign them to?

16. Does anything need to be communicated before the meeting?

## MANAGEMENT AND PLANNING TOOLS

This section is titled "Management and Planning Tools," but it could just as easily have been titled "Quality Tools and Techniques" because many of the tools and techniques come from the quality movement. We believe, however, that the title "Management and Planning Tools" more accurately reflects their purpose because each tool or technique enhances individual and group effectiveness by increasing the quality and speed of results. These outcomes are best achieved through planning and management practices. After all, as professionals, our goal is to produce the highest quality results in the shortest time possible. This gives us an additional competitive edge. These management and planning tools and techniques will assist you in achieving high quality results as well as providing you with resources that can generate innovation and creativity.

### THE TOOLS

We discuss eleven management and planning tools. Detailed resource information is supplied for each, covering how and when to apply the tool. The eleven tools are:

1. Pareto Chart
2. Classic Brainstorming
3. Brainwrite
4. Problem Solving
5. Affinity Diagramming
6. Tree Diagramming
7. Interrelationship Digraph
8. Matrix Diagram
9. Activity Network Diagram
10. Prioritization Matrices
11. Process Decision Chart

## PURPOSE

Planning tools save time, shorten the implementation cycle, and prevent expensive and time consuming rework. Management tools enhance results and increase levels of commitment.

## PROGRAM OBJECTIVES

At the completion of this program, participants will

- Understand the management and planning tools
- Be familiar with each tool and its application
- Be able to identify and appropriately apply each tool and technique
- Understand effective combinations of tools and techniques
- Gain insight into how management and planning tools can increase work group performance and effectiveness
- Learn "hands on" how to use six of the tools

## PARETO CHART

The first tool we will look at is called a Pareto. This tool is used for simple or complex applications. A Pareto chart is a special form of vertical bar graph that helps to determine which problems to solve and in what order. Doing a Pareto based upon various forms of data collection helps direct our attention and efforts to the more important problems. Usually, the impact for an organization is greater when we are able to address the highest value problems first. An example follows.

## **Problems with Meeting** Lateness

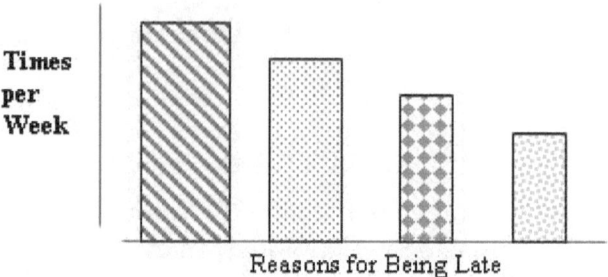

**Times
per
Week**

Reasons for Being Late

### WHEN TO USE

Pareto charting is a great tool for gathering information about a problem or condition. This works best when you need to display the relative importance of problems or conditions in order to:

- Choose a starting point for problem solving
- Determine simple prioritization
- View the data or information from different perspectives

### THE STEPS

1. Choose a problem to study
2. Choose the appropriate categories
   Existing information or reports can help provide the categories of causes or problems. Data must be collected and classified by the categories selected.
3. Select a unit of measure
   Data and problems can be viewed through a variety of measures. Frequency and cost to the customer or company are commonly used.
4. Choose a time periodThere is no set rule for choosing a time period. It usually depends upon the pace of the process, which is under examination. If more than one Pareto chart will be used for analysis, be sure your data collection periods are consistent for meaningful comparisons.

5. Gather the data
6. Compare the data collected

    For ease of comparison, enter and maintain the data in the appropriate way. This may be achieved with columns for the categories or measures chosen. This is the information to be represented in the Pareto chart.
7. Construct the Pareto Chart

    Draw the horizontal (x) and vertical (y) axes. Use the highest value in the measurement data set to determine the scale. Divide the scale proportionately using even multiples. Allow your data to determine the y-axis. Allow the range of data to determine the x-axis. Arrange the bars in descending order. Combine smaller bars if necessary. If you use software such as Microsoft Excel, the Pareto chart can be constructed automatically by using the chart function and by selecting the appropriate range of data.
8. Analyze and Interpret the results.

## CLASSIC BRAINSTORMING

Brainstorming has become an overly used term to mean a number of activities that are not brainstorming at all. It has come to mean any generic process of creating a set of ideas. Classic brainstorming is a very powerful tool that enhances the creativity and experience of a group.

### WHEN TO USE

Brainstorming can be used in many different situations, and it works well with other tools. It taps into the creative process of team members and generates free-flowing ideas or information around a topic.

### THE STEPS

1. **Agree on a Topic and Question**. The topic or question should be stated to encourage free thinking. Be sure the question or topic is not stated with a solution; this will direct the group's thinking too much. However, participants must understand the general purpose of the brainstorming session.

2.  **Idea Generation.** The more ideas the group can generate, the higher the probability they will find a breakthrough idea(s) that will help them succeed. Also, the greater the diversity within the group, the more diverse and creative the ideas will be.

    A good technique for starting the brainstorming process is the round robin method. This ensures participation by all members of the group. After two rounds, to generate more ideas open the meeting up to freewheeling participant contribution.

---

**Brainstorming Guidelines:**

1. List the ideas where they can be easily seen.
2. Do not make judgmental or value statements about ideas.
3. Passing is acceptable.
4. Building off other's ideas is encouraged.

---

3.  **Record Ideas.** Make sure all ideas are recorded as spoken. Be careful not to edit and interpret the ideas. Record the ideas where others can see them. This encourages building off others' ideas.

4.  **Check for Idea Exhaustion.** Keep the pace fast. Quick generation of ideas and connections helps to keep the energy high and ensures ideas will be captured before they are lost. Using two people to record ideas helps to keep the process moving.

5.  **Review the list of ideas.** Identify ideas that are virtually identical to another, and combine them into a single idea. This purging can be done during the brainstorming session or at a later time. Attempt to separate the list into logical components, such as things that can be easily done versus things that may be more difficult. When using classic brainstorming, the process can end at just reviewing the list of ideas. It is always a good idea to share the actionable outcomes of the brainstorm and their timing with the group that contributed to the brainstorm session.

## BRAINWRITE

This technique allows group members to continue brainstorming individually through writing. Sometimes during brainstorming, individuals will not share their ideas in front of a group. Brainwrite can extend the building effect during a brainstorming process as well as capture ideas from people who may not share them openly. It is also a powerful technique for building upon other ideas.

## WHEN TO USE

Brainwrite can be used as a stand-alone brainstorming process, or it can be used in conjunction with classic brainstorming. It is used for the same purpose as classic brainstorming.

## THE STEPS

1. Give each person a piece of paper (8.5 x 11) and have him or her tear it into four pieces.
2. Have each person record one idea on each piece of paper. Fold the piece, and place it in the center of the table.
3. Each person pulls one piece of paper at a time from the center pile and records at least one idea that builds on the idea(s) written on the paper. He or she then returns the folded paper to the center pile.
4. This process is repeated until each person has recorded at least one additional idea on each piece of paper.
5. When using Brainwrite as part of brainstorming, begin step 1 immediately following step 3 in the classic brainstorming process. When Brainwrite is completed, move to step 4 in the classic brainstorming process. You may want to record the results on a flip chart for everyone to see. If the list is long (and it will be), to save time consider having two people record the results.

# Problem Solving Model

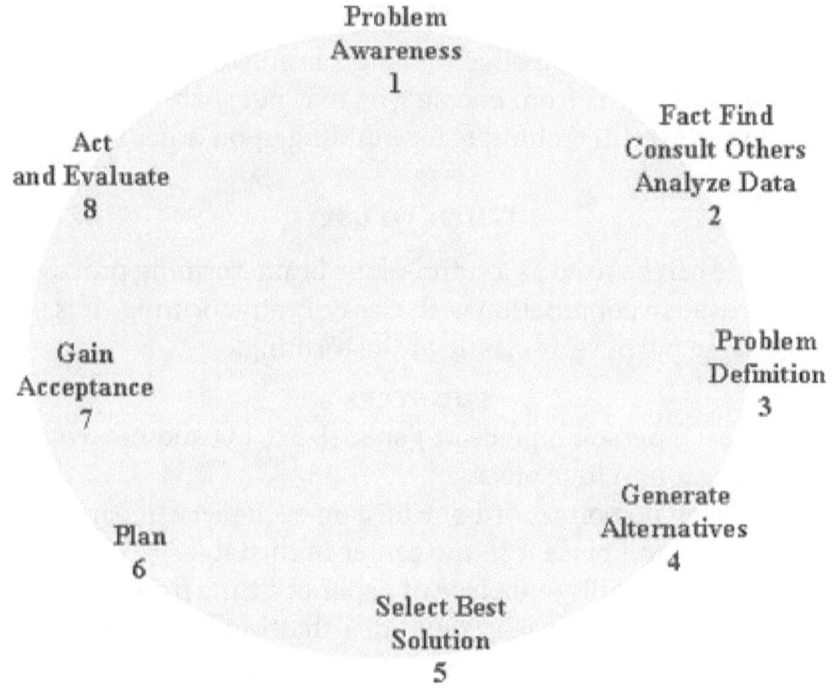

Problem
Awareness
1

Fact Find
Consult Others
Analyze Data
2

Act
and Evaluate
8

Problem
Definition
3

Gain
Acceptance
7

Generate
Alternatives
4

Plan
6

Select Best
Solution
5

### WHEN TO USE

Use for simple problem solving and medium complex problems. This model tends to increase quality, speed, and commitment to problem solving with groups. Individuals can use this model just as effectively as it can be used with groups.

### THE STEPS

#### 1. Problem Awareness

Problem situations are a normal part of organizations and life in general. We can sense or know through obvious or subtle and direct or indirect clues, that something is not right. This step may last for only a second, or it may stretch over a period of time. It is important not to react immediately and impulsively. It is also important to avoid doing nothing, hoping the warning signals you are receiving will go away. Once you are aware of a problem, move into step two.

## 2. Fact Find, Consult Others, Analyze Data

In this step you are seeking information to either firm up the problem or determine if it is worth addressing. This decision should be based upon data collected through talking with others involved or affected, data observed, and documentation collected. The choice not to solve a problem does not eliminate the problem. However, there are some problems we choose to live with and not solve. Once you have collected enough information, begin to analyze the data.

At this point, ask yourself the following questions:

- What do I know for sure about this problem?
- Do I have enough information to make a decision?
- Is there a perspective I may be overlooking?

If the data collected indicates you should deal with the problem, then move to *step three*.

## 3. Define the problem

A problem can be defined as the difference between the way something is and the way you want it to be or the way it should be. You must be able to describe the problem in some detail. The more specific you are in defining the problem, the less chance you have of dealing with a symptom. In defining the problem, it is usually helpful to describe the desired situation as opposed to the actual situation. This process may help you see the problem differently. There are three important rules for clearly defining a problem:

1. Separate problems from symptoms or possible solutions.

2. Avoid placing blame when identifying a problem. Focus on the problem and not the person or people.

3. Ask: What is really important?

When you clearly define the problem, you save time and resources that may be wasted dealing with a symptom. A clear problem statement provides the freedom to examine all aspects of the situation that may contribute to the problem. A sample problem statement may be:

### The problem is we don't have enough people.

This problem statement is too vague and assumes a solution. A more correct problem statement might be:

### Deliveries are not being made on time.

This problem statement reflects no symptoms or implied solutions. The reason deliveries are not on time may now be explored in greater detail and from a number of different perspectives. Naming a solution in the problem statement may narrow the fact-finding and thought processes to one area that may not be the problem at all. The problem may reside in the machinery, materials, conflicting priorities, the system, or the consequences of actions being taken.

### 4. Generate Alternatives

The obvious solution to a problem is not necessarily the one that will be the best solution. It is important to consider a full range of possible solutions prior to implementing one. A quick solution may cause us to deal with the same problem again at a later time. This is also the time when problem solvers consider whether this is a situation where there is only one right answer or many right answers.

At this point in the problem solving process, additional tools or techniques may need to be applied. Once a list of potential solutions is generated, you can move on to the next step in the model.

### 5. Select Best Solution

Now that you have generated your list of alternatives, you must compare the range of alternatives available against the specific limitations and risks involved, and select the best solution. In order to select the best solution, a set of criteria may be needed to assist with the selection process. This could be achieved by simply asking; "What do I want the solution to do?" This step should cause you to stop and consider the opportunity to achieve more than just solving the problem. This is where specific decision making occurs in the problem-solving process. When you choose a solution, you have completed the decision making aspect of problem solving.

## 6. Plan

The planning process is a matter of translating your chosen solution into action steps. The planning should provide a level of detail called "minimum critical specifications." In other words, don't plan any more details than you have to. Some plans require a great amount of input and detail. However, most of our daily problem solving requires little planning, and many times we don't even take the time to plan. Planning does not have to be time consuming, it can be quick and to the point. In any case, all plans should address the following:

### *Who What When Where How  (Why)*

Once you have a plan, it can be tested against the anticipated difficulties in implementing the plan or solution. The following five questions help prepare a plan for various difficulties.

1. What new problem might this solution create?
2. Where are the potential difficulties?
3. Who may be affected by this solution; who might benefit?
4. How might this solution be introduced?
5. When would be the best time to implement the solution?

## 7. Gain Acceptance

In the planning step you identified who might be affected by the solution. This step involves selling your solution to those individuals affected. If you have done a thorough job of planning, the task of convincing others should not be too difficult. If the solution affects people who were not involved in the problem-solving process thus far, you may have to work at getting them to understand the problem and the rationale for the solution selected, and you may have to work to gain their commitment to the solution. Above all, try not to surprise others with your solutions. Get key people involved in the problem-solving process up front.

This will save you extra work at this point of the process. Gaining acceptance also includes communicating the benefits and drawbacks of a solution. Again, if your planning reflects the appropriate level of detail, this information will already be available to share.

### 8. Act and Evaluate

We often make decisions by not making decisions. Not to decide is to decide. On the other hand, a predisposition to action can make a situation worse in the rush to do something. This is commonly known as "fire, aim, and ready." If we have completed the process to this point with care and clarity, the actions will be efficient and focused.

In this final step of the problem-solving process, measures of effectiveness are needed. The durability of how long problems stay solved is a critical measure of the solution's effectiveness. Another measure is whether learning occurred from the problem-solving experience. Some other measures are:

- Moving the present situation toward what you desire it to be
- Remaining applicable to the changing environment
- Evaluating other problems created from the solution
- Evaluating the smoothness of implementation

### AFFINITY DIAGRAM

The biggest obstacle to planning for improvement is past success or failure. It is assumed that what worked or failed to work in the past will continue to do so in the future. In changing work environments this assumption is limiting at best. We can use tools such as the affinity diagram to help break perpetuated patterns of thinking and to help us approach challenges and problems in new and creative ways.

The affinity diagram allows us to see problems or challenges in new ways and on different levels. It encourages true participation without using the traditional, time consuming discussion process, and it helps to encourage team involvement and support. An affinity process harnesses both creative and logical brain processes and focuses them on issues or problems.

## WHEN TO USE

The affinity diagram has proven to be helpful with nearly any situation. Don't limit yourself in its application. It works with simple or complex issues or problems. The cleanest application is in situations where facts or thoughts are chaotic or seem too complex to grasp or when breakthrough results are needed.

## MATERIALS NEEDED

The affinity diagram requires either Post-it notes or 5 x 7 cards for each participant. Markers used with overhead projectors are helpful because they are easy to read at a distance.

## THE STEPS

### 1. Assemble the Right Team

As with all tools and techniques, having the right people involved is instrumental to getting results. Typically, the more diverse a team is, the better it performs. A solid process keeps the team focused and on track.

### 2. Phrase the Issue to be Considered

It is best to state the issue in the form of a question. In order to encourage unbiased responses from team members, do not explain the issue or problem in much detail. The process works best when the issue is vaguely stated. You want to encourage a feeling of openness and "anything goes" when working the process. Give each participant a stack of 5 x 7 cards or Post-it notes and markers.

### 3. Generate and Record Ideas

Have participants print their information or responses on the card and limit them to one thought or idea per card. Print legibly and as large as the card will allow. Whenever possible, the statement should have a noun or a verb. This tends to make the statement less ambiguous.

## 4. Display the Completed Cards

Place the cards on the prepared wall, flip chart, or large table, and spread them out randomly. Be sure not to place any individual's responses together—mix them all up. Display the cards where everyone can see them. This will also keep participants engaged with the process.

## 5. Arrange the Cards into Affinity Groups

Affinity groups begin to form from the first pass. The first pass can be done by the facilitator or by a team member. Always make at least **three passes** at the affinity grouping. Have different people make each pass. This is a good way to get team members involved as well. If there is ever a strong disagreement concerning which group a card belongs to, defer to the owner of the card. Ask them what they meant when they wrote the card and where they think the card should go.

### AFFINITY EXERCISE INSTRUCTIONS

In order to practice the affinity diagram process, we have created an issue to be worked on by your assigned group.

**The Question:**     **What does _____ really value?**

Work the above question using the affinity diagram process.

When completed, choose a spokesperson from your group to present the findings to the class.

_____
_____
_____
_____

## Affinity Exercise II Instructions

In order to practice the affinity diagram process, we have created an issue to be worked on by your assigned group.

**Hat makes _____ a great place to work?**

1.     Answer the above question using the affinity diagram process.

2.     When completed, choose a spokesperson from your group to present the findings to the class.

_____

_____

_____

_____

_____

## Tree Diagram

The Tree Diagram systematically maps out, in increasing detail, the full range of paths and tasks associated with achieving the primary goal.  It serves to visually break down a complex issue or goal.  The Tree Diagram can be taken to various levels depending upon the main goal and the complexity of the problem or situation being worked.

### When to Use

**A Tree Diagram works well** when a task has been considered simple, yet has run into repeated roadblocks in implementation; when there are strong consequences for missing key tasks, such as safety or legal compliance issues; and when related tasks associated with a goal need to be identified.

## Sample Goal

### Purchase a high quality lawn mower

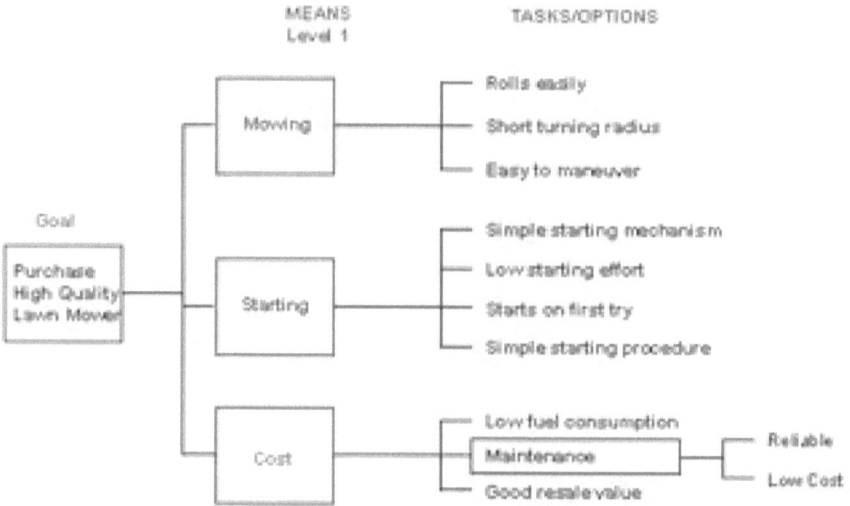

## 1. Choose the Tree Diagram Goal statement
The tree diagram starts with an overall goal, which is systematically
   broken down into the methods by which it will be achieved.
   The goal statement can come from any source. Three common
   sources are:
   • A root cause or effect from an interrelationship digraph
   • A key issue or header card from an affinity diagram
   • A team identified key issue or problem

## 2. Assemble the Right Team
   As with all tools and techniques, having the right people
   involved is very helpful in getting good results. The more
   diverse a team is the better it usually performs. In short,
   groups need processes to keep them focused and on track.

## 3. Generate the Major Tree Heading:
   • What needs to happen?
   • What needs to be addressed to resolve?
   • Achieve the Problem
   • Goal StatementWhen you have answered the question for
   the problem or goal statement, you have created the first level

of the tree diagram. The major outputs become the major tree headings. One of the most difficult things to do in constructing a Tree Diagram is to choose the right tree branches to explore. There is always the danger that we will use the traditional categories when many complex implementations require new paths of action.

**4. Complete the Tree Diagram Under Each Major Path**

A. Place the goal or problem statement to the extreme left of a flip chart or cards on a table. Ask the same question from step three for the next level of the diagram. Then choose the tasks or items that most directly relate to the first level objective. Remember, as you move from left to right in the tree the tasks are getting more and more specific. Therefore, the second level of detail should have a direct cause and effect relationship with the first level objectives.

B. Repeat the question for each level of implementation in the tree. It must be a direct tree because once the diagram is finished it should reflect all of the tasks to be completed for successful implementation.

**6. Review the Completed Tree Diagram for Logical Flow**

Ask the question: will these actions actually lead to these results? The diagram is effective only if the implementation of each level of detail really does accomplish the next higher level of tasks.

In order to practice the tree diagram process we have created an issue to be worked by your assigned group. In this case the course facilitator has already completed step two for you by assigning you to a group. Complete steps one through five on the goal presented below.

## Management and Planning Tools Glossary

**Affinity Diagram:** An affinity diagram organizes large amounts of information by grouping items that are similar.

**Brainstorming:** A method of shared problem solving in which all members of a group spontaneously contribute ideas.

**Brainwrite:** A method of shared problem solving in which all members of a group spontaneously contribute ideas in written form, building off each other's ideas.

**Criterion:** In the prioritization matrix, a criterion is the basis by which the different options will be judged in relation to the goal. There may be more than one criterion.

**Critical Path:** In an activity network diagram, the critical path determines the minimum time needed to complete the project and the relationships.

**Direct Relationships:** Relationships that you can see directly on a matrix diagram. A symbol is placed on the diagram to designate the relationships.

**Graphical PDPC:** A PDPC that is a combination of a tree diagram and a flow diagram.

**Header Cards:** In an affinity diagram, a card that best describes a grouping of similar cards.

**Indirect Relationships:** Relationships that you must infer; you cannot see the relationship explicitly because of the chart shape.

**Interrelationship Digraph:** A pictorial tool used to organize complex, multivariable problems or issues. It is used to study the relationships among elements of a problem and to identify the root causes or solutions.

**L-Shaped Matrix:** A matrix type that has two key considerations and includes only direct relationships.

**Sequential Flow:** In an activity network diagram, the longest path of sequential activities.

**Simultaneous Relationships:** In a matrix diagram, relationships that exist among all considerations simultaneously.

## REFERENCES

Certo, S. 1997. *Modern management.* Prentice-Hall, Upper Saddle River, New Jersey.

Covey, S. 1989 *The Seven Habit of Highly Effective People.* New York Simon & Schuster.

Drucker, P. 1954. *The Practice of Management.* New York. Harper.

Guest, E. 1976. *Collected Verse of Edgar Guest.* Cutchgue, New York. Buccanner Books.

Handy, C. 1985. *Understanding Organizations.* New York. Oxford University Press.

Heller, R. 2002. *Manager's Handbook.* Great Britain. DK.

Howard, P & J. 2001. *The Owner's Manual for Personality at Work.* Austin, TX. Bard Press.

Magretta, J. 2002. *What Management Is.* New York. The Free Press.

Moran, R & Stripp W. 1991. *Dynamics of Successful International Business Negotiations.* Houston, TX. Gulf Publishing

Moorhead, G & Griffin, R. 2001. *Organizational behavior.* Boston. Houghton Mifflin Company.

Sowell, T. 1983. *Ethnic America: A History.* Basic Books. New York.

Sulloway, F. 1997. *Born to Rebel.* Random House. New York.

Tichy, N. & Sherman, S. 1993. *Control Your Destiny or Someone Else Will: How Jack is Making General Electric the World's Most Competitive Corporation.* New York. Currency Doubleday.

**WEB SITES:**

HR Guide: **www.hr-guide.com**

International Stress Management Association

**www.stress-management.isma.org**

# Chapter Seven

## The Business Systems

## Keith Grant

Business is the mainspring of modern American life. It is the major economic activity in the country. It is the production and sale of goods and services by people for people. Business is the work people do to survive and more: to attain "the good life." Making a product or performing services are called business activities. Business activities are performed in many different kinds of organizations. These organizations are called business enterprises. Firms, companies, business concerns: these are synonyms for business enterprises. The incentive of business is private gain or profit. Business has other objectives as well, such as continued growth. Additionally, business may look for prestige in the community, or it may wish for public acceptance and liking.

It takes money to start a business and operate it. This money is called capital. In our society, business is financed primarily by private capital, and those who invest their capital expect a return on their investment: profit. Thus, in our society, private gain or profit is basic to business survival. Business can be understood in different ways. A recent development in the way many businesspeople view their activities is the so-called systems approach. In business, system means a situation or a problem is seen in its entirety—comprehensively—with all its integrated parts working together as a whole. This approach recognizes that a business is an organization of parts. Each individual part has its goals, but it works toward the common mission. This system approach is true at higher levels. The world of business is itself a whole made of business parts. Finally, an industry is composed of a group of firms that serve approximately the same group of buyers, and they offer products that are reasonably close substitutes for one another. Thus, we can speak of the banking industry, the automotive industry, or the fast-food industry. Industries may be classified in several ways. A very broad classification divides business into such groups as manufacturing and service.

## CHARACTERISTICS OF THE BUSINESS SYSTEM

Diversity is often found within the individual firm in the types of products produced or handled. A familiar example is the supermarket that sells not only groceries but clothes, hardware, and a variety of other items. There is even great diversity within a single product line of merchandise.

## INTERDEPENDENCE AND SPECIALIZATION

Increased diversity has been paralleled by greater interdependence among the elements of the business system. As America has grown, business activity has become more specialized. Companies that previously performed the activities of financing, production, engineering, human resources, and marketing under one management have given way to specialized firms that assist in various phases of these processes. As a result, firms become more dependent on one another. Dependence upon other business units is the natural outcome of specialization. A strike, inefficiency, or delay in any one segment of the chain of production highlights the sensitive interdependence of American business.

## DYNAMIC NATURE OF BUSINESS

The only certain thing about business is uncertainty; the only constant thing is change. From day-to-day and year-to-year, dynamic forces are at work. Some of these forces come from outside business: government regulations, wars, changing consumer taste, and new development in science and art, to name a few. From inside business there are new products and methods, innovations in management, and ceaseless competitive drive for customers' dollars that cause ever changing adjustments of polices and administration. And so, sales and costs fluctuate, net profits ebb and flow, and business firms come and go under the relentless pressure of change.

## FOUR MAJOR INFLUENCES OF ENVIRONMENT ON BUSINESS

The environment is the sum total of physical and social conditions influencing an individual and/or community. The business environment is the total of all things external to firms that affect them and how they are operated. The environment within that business influences its entire structure and component parts. In turn, business policies and practices have a reciprocal effect upon external forces. Business and its environment are interrelated and mutually dependent. American business has prospered with the framework of capitalism, a system that sanctions personal and property rights and generates individual initiatives.

Capitalism in its pure form is nonexistent, but the United States most closely approaches a market system in which competition dominates. In contrast, the communist nations approximate a command system, which has governmental or collective allocation and management of business resources. All business systems mix private rights and government controls to some degree. Modern socialism found in some nations usually reflects a midpoint between market and command systems.

In America, religious teachings are a source of strength and support in the conduct of business, with many of the drives and motivations in business behavior springing from many faiths giving approval to money-making. Attitudes of the public on morality and ethics serve as a check on business managers in pursuit of private gains. The social environment in business is becoming increasingly important, particularly the whole areas of environmental protection and quality of life. Corrective action must be taken by business or it will be forced to do so by outside elements.

## PROFIT-ORIENTED INSTITUTIONS

In this section I briefly summarize the various types of profit-oriented institutions in the United States. The goal of this section is to provide a quick reference to the reader and not to give a detailed explanation of each item.

Types of profit-oriented institutions

1. Sole proprietorships
2. Partnerships
3. Corporations

*Sole Proprietorship*

1. Constitute the majority of all business organizations but generate only about 10 percent of the profits.
2. Characteristics
   a. Easy to form
   b. No legal requirements
   c. Financing not complex
   d. Limited resale value
   e. No special tax status
   f. Owner managed
   g. Life of operation varies
   h. Business assets and personal assets are the same
   i. Unlimited flexibility

*Partnerships*

1. Two or more persons with complementary skills
2. Generally treated as sole proprietorship for most purposes

3. No legal requirements required but some sort of written is recommended
4. Types of Partnership
   a. Limited partnership has legal requirements in that they must be state approved, and the liability of each partner is limited to their contribution of capital
   b. Silent partnerships normally have certain members who contribute only capital to the setup
   c. Secret partnership usually have members who, for various reasons, are not to be known.

*Corporations*

1. Ownership is vested in shares of stock
2. It is a legal, artificial being
3. It is formed to protect the investor from unlimited liability
4. It is formed through Articles of Incorporation
   a. Issued by the state and forming the basic structure of the corporation
   b. Requires three or more people; the majority must be citizens
   c. Provides for a name and seal
   d. Sets forth the purpose of the organization
   e. Sets forth the financial structure
      1. Kinds of stocks
      2. Voting rights
   f. Defines the basic management
      1. Board of directors
      2. Bylaws formation
      3. Stockholder meeting, usually once a year

## THE FOUR FUNCTIONS OF MANAGEMENT

## PLANNING–FUNDAMENTAL

This section covers the four functions of management. Those functions are planning, organizing, leading and control. The first function is planning. Planning is a process. You set objectives, and then you figure out ways to achieve them. Planning is preparation for action. It implies a sensible concern for what may happen in the future and a disposition, by forehanded action, to forestall avoidable misfortune. Traditionally, planning is a management responsibility. Therefore planning consists of forecasting and having a design for meeting any unscheduled developments, favorable or otherwise, that may occur along the way. There are generally two stages in planning: The first phase is the conceptual step that consists of discussion, ideas, and trial schedules. The second step is the development stage that normally involves materials, people, and budgets. Planning is done before the activity. The first step is to survey the entire situation thoughtfully, to learn as much as possible about factors involved, and to think through what actions should be taken, in short, to plan. Long-range plans grapple with such issues as whether to market a new product, float a bond issue, restructure the organization, or merge or embark on an expansion program. Short-range plans usually consider operations and on-hand resources. Even the carefully laid plans backfire. Your plan should include objectives and goals.

Planning includes the following:

1. Determining what should be done
2. How it will be done
3. How long it will take
4. Where it should be done
5. Who should do it
6. Why they should do it

Generally there are two types of plans: long range (in the future) and short range (day-to-day). Administrative panning is usually long range based on: forecasts, expectation of future conditions, and needs. Operational planning is done at the lower levels in the organization and is generally less difficult, primarily, because it involves a shorter time span. It generally affects routines and processes.

## ORGANIZATION–FUNDAMENTAL

Organization implies a division of work, such divisions being called jobs and tasks (subdivision of jobs). It also implies that authority has been assigned at various levels in the organization. Organizing can be characterized as analysis and assignment. First, the organization analyzes the work to be done by determining the jobs and tasks that are necessary to carry out the plan that has been established. Next these jobs and tasks are assigned to individuals. Then the next step is to assign accountability and authority for completing the work. Without organization there is confusion and additional conflict. Activities that should be integrated and centralized are spread out and improperly led. Some individuals are overworked while others have little to do. Delays, duplications, and waste occur; expenses increase and talents and skills are not properly used. An individual initiative is lost, and morale suffers. With organization, each individual knows what his or her responsibilities and duties are. Necessary functions are determined and assigned so that personnel and physical facilities are utilized effectively.

Activities are coordinated. Confusion and conflict are minimized. When problems arise, individuals know where to seek solutions. In short, the organization is an integrated, coordinated group.

Everyone who is given responsibility for which they are accountable must be given the authority necessary to get results. Authority is the right to make, control, and enforce decisions. Authority must be clearly defined, both in extent (how much) and direction (even when). Although authority and responsibility can be delegated, the one who delegates is still accountable for the results. Without delegation of authority and responsibility, little could be accomplished. This decentralizes decision making; it pushes it down in the organization to a level near the point of action. Regardless of such delegation, however, each individual is accountable for their assigned responsibility. The identifying characteristic of planned organization is that it is an integrated, coordinated group, working effectively toward known objectives. A good organization operates effectively only to the extent that its people do. Also, it is based on functions, it is simple and easily understood, and it has stability, flexibility, balance, and capacity for growth.

## LEADING–FUNDAMENTAL

Leading is the relationship in which one person, the leader, influences others to willingly work together on related tasks to attain that which the leader desires. This means that anyone who is able to direct or influence others toward some common or shared position can function as a leader. The influence of a leader is of two different types. First, the leader owns performance, which directly affects the group level of work. An important part of this is the handling of authority and the subsequent relationships that the leader establishes. Second, there is the behavior the leader takes to affect the group's visibility and member's satisfaction, which is the basis upon which a leader influences a follower or a group of followers.

1. Coercive Power relies on fear and is based on the follower's expectation that punishment is given for not agreeing with a superior's actions and beliefs.
2. Legitimate Power is derived from the leader's position in the organization.
3. Reward Power means rewards are granted for compliance with a superior's actions and wishes.
4. Expert Power stems from an individual's possession of some special skills, knowledge, or expertise.
5. Referent Power is based on a follower's identification with a leader who is admired and held in high esteem.

The amount of interaction that should take place for good leadership to exist depends upon what is to be achieved, the behavior of the people involved, the knowledge and ideas that each can contribute toward solving a problem, and the permissiveness of the general environment. A leader leads but does not push. The leader pulls followers to heights of accomplishments they may not have believed were possible. A leader knows the individual characteristics of key followers, knows what qualities will elicit their best efforts, and serves at the same time he or she leads. The leader has the ability to awaken emotional as well as rational powers of the followers. Leading is getting all the members of the group or organization to want and strive to achieve mutual objectives. The principle of leading is that favorable actuating efforts are normally obtained by treating employees as human beings, encouraging their growth and development, instilling a desire to excel, recognizing work well done, and insuring fair play.

Listed below are some general personal and managerial traits that are used by a leader:

**Personal Traits**
1. Intelligence is the ability to think clearly and concisely about business and its problems.
2. Open-mindedness is absorbing new ideas and other points of view.
3. Emotional stability is the avoidance of moodiness, inconsistency, and the intrusion of personal feelings.
4. Skill in handling people requires an awareness of others ideas and motives, and requires an ability to develop firm, pleasant relations with associates or followers.
5. Acceptance of responsibility
6. A dynamic approach to problems and ideas—the seeking of new ideas and ways of doing things, plus a willingness to test and use them.
7. An ability to communicate and express oneself clearly in the spoken or written word.

**Managerial Traits**
1. A managerial point of view: a capacity for analyzing policy problems on a broad basis.
2. An understanding of and appreciation for the company-wide interrelationship.
3. A sense of the social responsibilities of business leaders to the industry, the community, and the nation.
4. A full understanding of social, political, and economic forces that influence the policy decisions of leadership.
5. A deep appreciation of the human problems within organizations, along with the ability to deal effectively with people.
6. An understanding of the complexities inherent in labor–management relationships.

7. Belief in the value of education and training as a lifetime pursuit.

## CONTROL–FUNDAMENTAL

Control is comparing performance with standards—feedback. Control is defined as the function of regulating action in relation to the plan. It involves setting up criteria or checks, comparing actual results with those criteria, and making needed corrections. Because control constrains and regulates, it maybe a less popular management function than others. It is not always pleasant or easy to apply needed controls. However, without such application, results maybe inadequate.

**Objectives of control—the primary purposes of control are to:**

1. Assure that performance follows the established plan
2. Coordinate action
3. Minimize waste
4. Ensure that goals and standards are met

**Prerequisites of Control**

Not everything needs controlled. Often, if one aspect of a situation is controlled, other aspects will fall into place. Thus, the key to control is to determine the strategic factor. Control and communications are interrelated. Controls often break down simply because someone has not fully understood the problem and/or the process involved. What may appear to be a clerical error may, in reality, be a communication error—the employee did not know what was supposed to be done or how it was supposed to be done. The problem of communication has many facets. First, words themselves are awkward. Shades of difference among meanings are often slight and colored by an individual's experiences and environment. Communication is further complicated by a reservoir of emotions and attitudes, generally unconscious, which profoundly affect communication. This is sometimes referred to as the emotional climate of communication. Finally, timing of a statement makes a difference. Stating issues at the right place and proper is a critical element of timing.

Authority is essential to maintain control. Without standards, there is no basis for comparison. One aspect of control, particularly of production control, is comparison. The comparison may be with a time standard, performance, cost, or a set of quantitative criteria.

Standards presuppose measurement. If something can be measured, standards can be set; and if standards can be set, control can be enforced. Standardization of criteria is an important aspect of control because it creates consistency.

## Organization Structures

There are two types of organizations: planned (formal) and unplanned (informal). Even when organizations are formally planned according to the best guidelines, there will always be an informal organization. Natural leaders sometimes have more influence than designated, or positional, leaders. Integrating them is part of the management process in constructing the framework for a healthy, viable organization. There are three basic forms of organization structure: line, functional, and line and staff. Each structure spells out the authority and responsibility relationship in an organization. The essence of each kind of organizational structure is its authority and responsibility relationship. Line authority is the right to lead. Functional authority is line authority over a specialized area. Staff authority is the right to advise and recommend.

### *Line structure*

A line structure is one in which authority flows vertically, in a direct line from the highest executive to the lowest employee. It is the simplest and oldest form of organization. In business, the pure line form of organization is usually found only during early stages of development. A single proprietor with only one or two employees can very well operate a line structure because problems are relatively simple.

## Advantages and Disadvantages

A line organization is simple and easily understood. Each employee knows who his or her leader is and who has authority to issue orders. Because authority flows in a direct line from leader to employees, it is fairly easy to determine accountability for nonperformance, failure to pass along instructions, or failure to carry out orders. A line organization provides for rapid decision making. This is especially true if problems are not complex. Each executive has full authority for decisions in areas of leadership. A line organization can be economical for a small business, because it limits the number of executives and requires no specialists. There is no specialization; hence, any professional helps unless a consulting firm is called in. A line organization places too much responsibility on the top executive.

## *Functional Structure*

The foundation of a functional structure is specialization. That is, the work is planned and carried out on a functional basis with a specialist in charge of each function. The specialists have line authority over his or her function throughout the organization. A human resources manager, for example, is the company's designated specialist in human resources matters. The office manager is the functional specialist in office matters, regardless of where office work is done.

## Advantages and Disadvantages

The function organization is built around experts. Each supervisor or staff or person is an expert in their field. There are several disadvantages in a functional structure. Authority and accountability are divided. Each work has a number of leaders.

## *Line and Staff Structure*

A line organization develops generalists: individuals who can execute and lead in different areas. The authority of the specialist is, however, advisory, not functional.

Advantages and Disadvantages

In general, a line and staff organization retains the advantages of both line and functional organizations. In it, authority and responsibility are fixed: each individual reports to only one leader, but specialized help is available from the staff experts through the line executive. Technical problems are handled by the specialists. There is a tendency for staff leaders to take over line authority. Naturally, a staff person wants to see his or her ideas put into effect, and they may try to force these ideas on line personnel. Decisions may be slowed by the line executives who unduly rely upon staff advice and recommendations.

## Committee Structure

Although some individuals consider the committee as a fourth form of organization, it is most commonly used as a supplement to the three forms discussed above. Committees have a very definite place and significance in organizational structure. They are, in fact, a form of a staff organization, established to render specialized advice or to obtain a meeting of the minds.

Advantages and Disadvantages

They are useful in determining policies, in coordinating plans, in taking disciplinary actions, in pooling ideas, in training line executives, and in cutting across departmental lines. The chief limitations are that they are time consuming, and one individual may dominate the discussions. The committee may spend time on irrelevant material, or decisions reached may be poor because they were influenced by a particularly articulate or persuasive member of the committee.

This brief summary is provided as a primer on basic business terms. One of the keys is providing useful and meaningful information. Having a common understanding of terms and how they are used is necessary to have a meaningful discussion.

## REFERENCES

Drucker, P. (1990). *Managing the Nonprofit Organization.* CollinsBusiness, New York.

Jonnard, C. (1998*). International Business and Trade.* St. Lucie Press, New York.

Maxwell, J. (2002). *The Maxwell Leadership Bible.* The Thomas Nelson, Nashville, TN.

# NOTES

# About the Authors

**Janis McFaul, PhD**

Janis has twenty-three years of experience at GM. She joined Enterprise Customer Management (ECM) in April 2001 after holding the position of *Director of e-Marketing* in Tokyo, Japan, for two years (February 1999 – March 2001). At General Motors Japan, Janis was responsible for five business units including, Market Research, Call Center, Customer Relationship Management, Web Development, and Business & Competitive Analysis.

As the international lead within ECM, Janis is responsible for overall support for General Motors global marketing locations in regard to Customer Relationship Management (CRM). She is charged with supporting the regions by sharing global best practices and by supplying training opportunities internationally via the General Motors University CRM course, which she codeveloped.

Janis has worked in the field of international marketing at General Motors for the past fifteen years. Her assignments included business manager for the Australian Holden Project, international brand manager for Corvette and mid-size Van, and field marketing manager for the Caribbean.

In addition to her work with General Motors, Dr. McFaul is an adjunct professor at University of Phoenix (Detroit Campus) and Lawrence Technology University. She also taught International Marketing for McGill University when she was living in Tokyo.

After graduating from business school, Janis decided to go on to pursue her doctorate in marketing and cultural anthropology. She wrote her doctoral dissertation on the international application of relationship marketing.

## Keith B. Grant

Keith has held various managerial positions at General Motors. He has taught at various colleges and universities. Students voted him the most outstanding graduate instructor in 1998, 2000, and 2001. He has a PhD in organizational behavior from the Union Institute and University. He has published two other books, *Sentenced in the Womb* (2000) and *Birth Order in the Workplace* (1997)

## Jeanette Pack and Ionie Douglas

Jeanette Pack, DM, and Ionie Douglas, DM, are recent graduates from the University of Phoenix (UOP) doctoral program in leadership. Both have undergraduate degrees in nursing.